The Letters of Peter H. Burnett

Realism and the Roots of California

Perceptions

"The problem is, Burnett was a staunch racist who supported the exclusion of blacks from the state, the suspension of Chinese immigration and the extermination of Native Americans."—huffingtonpost.com/2011/05/19

[Peter Burnett was] "...a little too slow in action and too wordy in speech for quick-witted men of deeds; a little too conservative..." —Hubert Howe Bancroft, iconic nineteenth century Far West historian, 1888

"California's first Governor bluntly advocated Indian genocide by declaring: 'A war of extermination will continue to be waged between the races until the Indian race becomes extinct' " —Edward Castillo, Indian historian, author, 1999.

"Mr. Burnett was unquestionably the most intelligent lawyer then in the country [Oregon]. He was a very ambitious man—smooth, deceitful, and insinuating in his manners."—William Henry Gray, historian, 1870.

"...Peter Burnett, the state's first governor and *pro-slavery* Democrat."(emphasis added) —Hon. Joseph R. Grodin, associate justice, California Supreme Court 1982-1987, 2008.

[after uncovering] "the chilling details... I called the superintendent and I said, 'We need to change the name of that school [Burnett Child Development Center]'.... There was a great team effort in the community after I sounded the alarm." —Rev. Amos Brown, NAACP chapter president, 2011.

"...Peter H. Burnett, California's first governor, remains an important figure not only in the political history of California but in its intellectual history as well...[His] letters reveal a Founder who epitomizes what the California-born philosopher Josiah Royce described as the Higher Provincialism emerging from the first frontier." —Kevin Starr, California State Librarian 1994-2004, 2013.

"Judge Burnett, a Western man of the highest character, was nominated for Governor...." —Francis J. Lippitt, pioneer and author, 1849.

"...Burnett stands in the first rank of nineteenth century American Catholic apologists." —Avery Cardinal Dulles, 2004.

"What strikes the reader at a glance in this remarkable volume [Burnett's book] is its perfect honesty and sincerity" —Orestes Brownson, leading American philosopher, 1860.

The Letters of Peter H. Burnett

Realism and the Roots of California

Editor
Dominic Colvert

Solas Press
Antioch
2013

Copyright © 2013 Solas Press
All rights reserved

Library of Congress Cataloging-in-Publication Data

Burnett, Peter H. (Peter Hardeman), 1807-1895.
 The letters of Peter H. Burnett : realism and the roots of California / editor, Dominic Colvert.
    pages cm
 Includes bibliographical references and index.
 Summary: "Provides new and surprising information about the founding of the state of California"--Provided by publisher.
 ISBN 978-1-893426-75-7
 1. Burnett, Peter H. (Peter Hardeman), 1807-1895--Correspondence. 2. California--History--1846-1850. 3. California--Politics and government--1850-1950. 4. Governors--California--Biography. 5. Legislators--Oregon--Biography. 6. Frontier and pioneer life--Oregon. 7. Pioneers--Oregon--Correspondence. 8. Pioneers--California--Correspondence. I. Colvert, Dominic, 1932- II. Title.
 F864.B957 2013
 979.4'04092--dc23
 [B]
                                                                               2013015345

Manufactured in the United States of America

Peter H. Burnett

1807 – 1895

Table of Contents

Preface ix

Part 1: Prologue

I Historical significance of the letters	3
II Outline of Burnett's life	9
III Interactions with Californian Indians	19
IV Interactions with African Americans	25
V The Archy case	30
VI Burnett's persona and the influx from China	38
VII Conclusions	41

Part 2: Lawyer, Newspaper Editor, 1833-1843

1836 August 11, editorial: THE NEXT SESSION OF THE LEGISLATURE	47
1836 August 18, editorial: LAND OFFICE MONEY	51
1836 September 8, editorial: The editor of the "MONITOR"	54
1836 September 22, editorial: THE TREATY	56

Part 3: Explorer, Farmer, Legislator, Judge, 1843-1848

1844 January, letter to editor, New York Herald	61
1844 January, letter to editor, New York Herald	68
1844 January, letter to editor, New York Herald	73
1844 January, letter to editor, New York Herald	78
1844 January, letter to editor, New York Herald	84
1844 November 2, letter to J. White, sub-Indian agent	91
1844 November 4, letter to *Living Age* magazine	94
1847 October 27, letter to James M. Hughes	97

1848 November 8, letter to editor, *California Star*   108

Part 4: Gold Miner, Political Advocate, Business Agent, 1849

1849 January 8, letter to editor *Alta California* (As President of the Committee)   113

1849 April 20, letter to editor, *Alta California*   116

1849 June 18, letter to editor, *Alta California*   121

1849 July 5, letter to editor, *Alta California*   123

Part 5: Governor of California, 1849-1850

1850 June 1, letter to Major General Bean   131

1850 June 4, letter to Major General Bean   133

1850 August 15, letter to Brigadier General A. Winn   134

1850 September 4, letter to Major General Bean   135

1850 October 25, letter to Sheriff William Rogers   136

1850 November 13, letter to Brigadier General Winn   137

1850 November 15, letter to Sheriff William Rogers   138

1850 November 15, letter to Brigadier General Winn   139

Part 6: Lawyer, 1850-1857

1852 April 26, letter to Mr. Buckley   143

1852 September 6, letter to Mr. Cist   144

1855 August 13, letter to Rev. Fr. Congiato, S.J.   145

Part 7: Author, Supreme Court Judge, 1857-1862

1859 May 17, letter to Bishop Purcell   149

1859 December 1, letter to Bishop Purcell   152

1859 December 25, letter to Bishop Purcell   153

1860 January 3, letter to Orestes Brownson	155
1860 January 25, letter to Bishop Purcell	157
1860 February 2, letter to Bishop Purcell	159
1860 March 29, letter to Bishop Purcell	162
1860 June 8, letter to Orestes Brownson	165
1860 June 22, letter to Bishop Purcell	166
1860 December 28, letter Bishop Purcell	169
1861 February 9, letter to editor, *Alta California*	171
1861 February 13, letter to Bishop Purcell	179
1862 July 16, letter to a candidate for Congress	181

Part 8: Bank President, 1862-1880

1873 February 18, letter to cousin	185
1873 March 19, letter to Cousin Glen	186

Part 9: Author, Retiree. 1880-1895

1883 May 21, letter to Paxton Cole	191
1885 March 11, letter to a family member	193
1888 September17, letter to Cousin Glen	194
1889, Preface, *A Chaplet of Verse*	196
1890 October 6, letter to nephew	199
1891 May 21, letter to a nephew	200

APPENDIX

Exhibit A, THE INAUGURAL ADDRESS	203
Exhibit B, THE GOVERNOR'S MESSAGE OF 1851	215
Index of Names	243

Editor's Preface

The nineteenth century was the political cauldron in which American society was articulated. Burnett's letters have the power to present an unvarnished view of those world-shaping events. Beyond painting an intimate portrait of a founding father they, casting light as they do on the events and historical actors, provide important clues to the heady questions: What was it like then? How did we come to be as we are? And what worked well for the nation?

Apart from the historical story, Peter Burnett led a very adventurous life, beginning as he did in poverty and succeeding in becoming a historical actor of importance. In addition, the poor press he receives is difficult to harmonize with his well recorded spiritual quest—for as Thomas Merton noted, "Charity is neither weak nor blind. It is essentially prudent, just, temperate, and strong." These are some of the many topics that make it impossible not to be stirred to curiosity.

In editing the letters, I have tried to give exactly what was written and not offered corrections of any kind, except adding some paragraphing and punctuation. Of course, as with all handwritten documents, the peculiarities of the author's handwriting and the quality of the reproduction offered challenges.

I offer a special thanks to the archivists in the various institutions whose generous help made this volume possible. It is to be hoped that its publication will spur the discovery of more of his correspondence in other collections or private hands.

Dominic Colvert

Part 1
Prologue

I
Historical significance of the letters

Peter H. Burnett, as he usually signed his letters, was the first civil governor of the state of California that was carved from the Mexican province of Alta California. The letters given here include private letters to individuals and those directed to the public through the media. Moreover, given in an appendix are his addresses to the California Legislature in 1849 and 1851, since these shed light on his letters.

While a fuller assessment of Burnett must await a biographical study, the material will reveal the intellect and character of a founding father as well as a unique view of the living conditions at the roots of modern California. To those familiar with well received views of Burnett and his times, the material will supply new and surprising information.

Unearthing a new and surprising aspect of history gives a thrill to the historian and non-specialist alike, but history has a higher, or at least broader, function. It has an essential role in creating the present. Despite progressivist aberrations that traditions and social norms can be neglected, ultimately it is culture and its transcendent notions of love of neighbor, the common good, human dignity, and so on that shapes the civic reality. As the philosopher Kevin Wall noted, "The myth is what makes social cohesion possible."[1]

Primitive societies had creation myths where a divine irruption instituted the tribe. These creation myths had the power to sway warriors to nobly sacrifice their individual existence for the life of the tribe. Similarly, roots and traditions—what Eric Voegelin calls "the symbols by which political societies interpret themselves"—provide modern societies and California with the *trans-historical meaning* necessary for unity and individual sacrifices for the common good.[2] A knowledge of the state of affairs in the nineteenth century with the

---

[1] Kevin Wall, former professor at the Dominican School of Philosophy and Theology at the Graduate Theological Union, Berkeley, in an unpublished lecture.

[2] Eric Voegelin, *The New Science of Politics: An Introduction* (Chicago: The University of Chicago Press, 1952), 1.

many anxiety provoking issues of that day adds a dimension to the thinking about similar problems today. Indeed, a broad spectrum of issues such as justice for minorities, the collective response to intergenerational debt, and the conduct of war, are prefigured in that period.

There will be, of course, difficulties in appraising the issues within the context of Burnett's life and times. Unlike the sciences that deal in universals that can command a level of unanimity, history deals with singular and contingent events that lend themselves to dialectally plausible but contrary interpretations. In the challenge to telling what happened, the primary documents given here, particularly the private letters will be of great assistance.

Readers of the letters will need to place themselves mentally in the nineteenth century as they attempt to reach beyond raw facts and discover something of Burnett's hidden inspiration that is the essential measure of character. And beyond the ambiance of the letters, an appreciation of general conditions is needed. In civic affairs, President James K. Polk's expansionist policies at mid-century were then controversial.[3] On social issues, we read now with utter incomprehension of the ubiquity of the "cat-o'-nine-tails" for discipline on land and at sea, and that anyone could lose their liberty in various forms of indentured service. Some understanding is needed of the hard-scrabble existence on the frontier, the settlers' attitude that whatever ground they chose was their property, the warring Indian tribes, and the black race denied human dignity. And although the historical facts about governance are clear, it is difficult to grasp that the Union, the United States of America as we know it, was not then secure. The hegemony of the U.S. in the Far West was far from certain, opinions on the proper extent of U. S. territory varied. In 1839 John Sutter had shown that California was a prize that could go to an enterprising filibusterer or nation, and in 1844 a mere eight hundred peaceable settlers had secured Oregon from British rule.

There are, as well, difficulties peculiar to *our* era. In modern times there has been an attempt to move away from the tendency to glorify heroic beginnings and move to a scientific, extensively factual, non-

---

[3] Burnett was related through marriage to President Polk, but this did not prevent his criticism of Polk's policies; see the letter April 20, 1849.

sentimental view of history.[4] While striving to compose a narrative of "what actually happened," this method inevitably moves the historic to the *historical*. Another threat to a balanced view lies in viewing these old events through a political lens or through politically sanctioned histories. It seems also, that there is a timeless part of human nature with a biasing effect—it was reportedly Socrates in the fifth century B.C. who said, "The children of the present age have no respect for their elders." Indeed, despite the noble aspirations of critical thinking to avoid hagiographic accounts, there is, in reality, a rival development that places an unbalanced accent on the *barbarous* activities of our ancestors.

Unfortunately, modern California's roots in the 1849 Gold Rush had more than a fair share of barbarism. Stories of what someone has called "murder for amusement," emphasize the lurid violence of the period. Narratives of lynchings, accounts of dueling, descriptions of old San Francisco's red light district, known as the Barbary Coast, all so reprehensible, leave indelible impressions of savagery and moral decadence. Burnett astutely noted that it was a society lacking the civilizing influence of women. But the good and heroic existed alongside the others. For example, Burnett recounts, on arrival at Longs Bar in November 1848, the miners left their gold in their unattended tents without incident during the day. At the beginning of the Gold Rush the solution to dealing with malcontents in the absence of civic authority was banishment from the neighborhood. As is found in the often repeated story of the Donner Party, their tragic entrapment in the snowy mountains elicited noble and daring rescue efforts as well as the worst in human nature.

Transporting ourselves back in spirit to the Far West in the nineteenth century, it will be obvious that conditions were not favorable for keeping records. As a case in point, the first governor governed from hot and humid make-shift quarters in San Jose. Luckily, some of his letters from each stage in his long life have survived.

The first of Burnett's letters obtainable are the series of letters published in the *New York Herald* beginning on the fifth of January 1845, written when he was thirty-six years of age. These letters were

---

[4] The Historical Critical Method. See Gilbert Garraghan, *A Guide to Historical Method* (New York: Fordham University Press, 1957).

PROLOGUE

extracted by the *Herald* from a more extensive manuscript provided to the editor by Burnett's marvelous account of the iconic Oregon Trail Emigration of 1843. The manuscript was edited by James Gordon Bennett, the renowned editor of the *Herald*, and the primary material appears to be lost. In later years, Burnett kept files of his correspondence, but unfortunately the riches that these files promise have, according to his great-great-granddaughter, been lost to us through a blunder by a storage company.

This question of what James Gordon Bennett received and published was taken up by Fredric Young in 1902. He notes:[5]

> ...Burnett says [in his memoirs]: "I kept a concise journal of the trip as far as Walla Walla, and have it now before me." The last date on the journey given in the letters is June twenty-seventh. Yet it seems almost certain that the copy sent by Burnett to the *Herald* covers the whole trip. One reason for this inference is found in Burnett's statement of the amount of copy he sent—"some hundred and twenty-five pages of foolscap..."

Another notable observation by Young concerns a book, *History of Oregon*, published in New York in 1845 by George Wilkes. Young says:

> ...Statements by Wilkes concerning the author and the character of the material used by him in Part II of his book, along with indubitable internal evidence, prove conclusively that the whole Burnett manuscript sent to the *New York Herald*, part of which was printed in the *Herald*...was the basis of Wilkes' book.

Prior to composing the Oregon migration saga on "some hundred and twenty-five pages of foolscap" for the readers of the *Herald*, Burnett had the opportunity in 1837 to shed light on his perspective on government and civic affairs. He was a newspaper editor at age twenty-nine. It is possible to appraise Burnett's personal opinion and philosophy from his selection of materials and in the editorials he composed. While it is to be expected that editorials would employ a more guarded presentation than a private letter, they are practical in showing the development of his ideas. As will be seen, the lessons he

---

[5] Fredric George Young, ed., *The Quarterly of the Oregon Historical Society*, Vol. III, March 1902—December 1902: 398.

learned as editor of *The Far West* in Missouri influenced his governing in California.

As is evident from the letters here and other sources, Burnett led a very adventurous physical, intellectual, and spiritual life. It is beyond question that he was a good family man, fair in his dealings with others, courageous in action, and that he had the capability of interacting well with men of high caliber. In addition, it is well known that in both his siblings and immediate family there were many examples of legislators, ministers of religion, military and commercial men of note. Peter H. Burnett exhibited a high-minded philosophic approach to constitutional law, and in his lifetime helped bring the distinct benefits of a Yankee republican government to California. A partial list of his remarkable actions taken in collaboration with other historic figures might include:

- Organizing and being the first captain of the iconic Oregon migration from Missouri.
- Reorganization of the Oregon laws.
- Organizing and being captain of the wagon train that blazed the trail for immigrants from Oregon to California.
- Being a major influence in California's Constitutional Convention.
- Serving as California's first governor.
- Restoring before the Civil War California's status as a free state by negating the California Supreme Court ruling that the anti-slavery article of the Constitution was inoperative.
- Authoring a book that Avery Cardinal Dulles said places him "in the first rank of American Catholic apologists."

California's state librarian, Kevin Starr, describes Burnett's work in California as "a case study in the fast-forwarding of history that was the California Gold Rush," and in regard to his writing says:

> Burnett does not write...as a frontiersman, nor even a provincial. Like the great Puritan divines of seventeenth-century Massachusetts, he writes with full authority and

assurance, trusting his sources, unintimidated by the prestige of his intellectual opponents.[6]

With such a pedigree, it would seem that his positive place in California history is needed and assured, but this is not the case. Reviewing what has been written on Burnett will show a lot of marshaling of facts for opinionated accounts.

Making judgments about motivation in historical situations is complex. For it is one thing to be opposed to, say, Burnett's idea that Chinese immigration needed to be limited, or opposed to his imposition of a poll tax, and quite another thing to show that he was not just wrong but motivated by xenophobia or small-mindedness. To move seamlessly from policy analysis to *ad hominems* would be to engage in mindless dialectic or to descend to politicking. There are many examples of such incongruities in the literature, as well as the more egregious use of selective quotations.

It is natural, in the chaos of his times and with his meteoric rise from poverty and humble beginnings, that Burnett, a man of sound legal reasoning, an analytical mind, and given to offering his opinions fearlessly, would have hard-hitting differences with contemporaries. Furthermore, while in his writings *he* never exceeds a gentlemanly rebuke, it is to be expected that there will be others less temperate in their judgments of him. Indeed, in the normal course of events some will be found to be maliciously motivated. So it is not surprising, whether true or not, that there are accusations of a militant xenophobia and of a deceitful character.

---

[6] Kevin Starr, foreword, *The True Church: The Path that Led a Protestant Lawyer to the Catholic Church* (Antioch, California: Solas Press, 2004), x.

II

Outline of Burnett's life

The following brief outline of his life will provide a useful prelude to reading these letters.[1] Peter Hardeman Burnett was born in Nashville, Tennessee on November 15, 1807, the third child in a struggling but stable family. His father, George, was a carpenter, and his mother, the former, Dorothy Hardeman, was the daughter of a well-to-do farmer.

Probably through a desire for upward mobility, and in an astute evaluation of his son's aptitudes, his father early on encouraged the young boy to study law. Neither of his parents, though nominally Baptists, appears to have been overtly religious. But he learned tribal maxims from his maternal grandfather about the importance of family loyalty and paying debts. He practiced these maxims to the end of his life.

Helped by the Hardeman in laws, the family moved twice before Peter was ten years old. They arrived in Howard County, Missouri, in 1817. In 1822 the family moved again to escape the unhealthy climate of their river-bottom farm in Howard County. This time they moved to a farm close to Liberty, in Clay County, Missouri. His older sister, Constantia married Major William Smith in July 1823. Peter admired his sister, and shortly after the marriage he moved to live in Liberty with his sister and brother-in-law. There he learned the rudiments of frontier trading from Major Smith.

As a callow youth of nineteen he set out from Clay County in the fall of 1826 with his worldly possessions of $26, a new suit made by his mother, and a rather weak pony to seek his fortune in Tennessee. In a testament to family cohesion, his leaving his immediate family was done under the tutelage and assistance of his uncle Constant Hardeman. His emergence from the family bosom was a seminal event in his life. His eyes were opened when he compared his frontier existence to his cousins' wealth, living conditions, and, more important, the books and literature available to them. He immediately resolved to improve himself.

---

[1] The State of California purports to provide such a summary on its website, but the piece adopts a juvenile tone and is wholly ambiguous. See http://governors.library.ca.gov/01-Burnett.html. 2012/12/10.

PROLOGUE

After visiting with Constant Hardeman's family in Rutherford County for a short time, he set out with his uncle Blackstone Hardeman, who was moving to a new farm near Bolivar, Missouri a town named by the many settlers from Bolivar, Tennessee. By Christmas of that year his uncle found employment for him in that raw frontier town as a clerk in a hotel being developed. His work was really to be a general factotum, but his cheerful attention to duties drew the attention of the Reverend W. Blount Peck. In May of the following year Peck invited him to clerk in his new store at Clear Creek, some fifty miles to the northwest.

Peter Rogers moved with his wife and two young daughters to Clear Creek in the fall of 1827. Burnett had a friend, Calvin Stephens, who dated their eldest daughter, sixteen-year-old Harriet Rogers. In a spirit of mischievousness he decided to try to "cut-out" his friend who he felt had superior "looks and refinements." He succeeded beyond his expectations, and he and Harriet made their lifetime vows and were wed in August 1828. Before he was twenty-two his first child was born, and he had purchased the Reverend Mr. Peck's trading business in the spring of 1829.

The young man's time as a business proprietor at Clear Creek resulted in life-altering experiences. One such event occurred in 1830 when a burglar forced entry to his store to steal liquor. Burnett's response was to sleep in the store with a loaded shotgun. However, he was chagrined to find that he had slept soundly throughout an attempted break-in, and he decided to booby-trap the entry point. Before departing for home in the evening he carefully arranged a system of cords so that the forcing of a window shutter would fire the shotgun. On arrival at the store in the morning he found the burglar dead, killed instantly by the shot entering his forehead. The memory of this sad experience haunted him, for we find him writing in his memoirs, "I would rather bear almost any injury than take human life." It undoubtedly contributed to the aversion he exhibited later to both war and dueling. He also developed a superstition about the evils of liquor, believing that his luck was poor when he became involved with the sale or manufacture of it. So later in Oregon he was a prime mover in introducing restrictive liquor laws that were to persist in spirit in Oregon legislation.

Trading on the frontier was largely a matter of credit management, requiring shrewd judgments about people and economic conditions. Whether because of his former boss's well timed sale or Burnett's mismanagement or the economic climate, the business did poorly. In this situation Burnett resolved to follow his father-in-law, who had moved to Clay County, Missouri, and as a back-up plan, he "purchased the books" and he and his wife's cousin began their independent study of law in their spare time. Within three years of becoming the owner of the store he was unable to collect on the IOUs for goods sold, and the business collapsed. Penniless and desperate, he fled to his father-in-law's home in Clay County in April 1832. There Harriet and his child had already sought refuge.

The next ten years he spent in Clay County were hectic with failures and triumphs. Harriet bore him five more children. Beginning as a store clerk in Liberty, he moved on to entrepreneurial business ventures on borrowed capital. For whatever reason, Dame Fortune did not smile on those endeavors. Apart from the questions about his business acumen and whether he was guilty of the common enough overweening confidence of that time and place, there was the fact that the American economy was engulfed by the ruinous Panic of 1837. Among financial crises, that of 1837 is counted as momentous; so much so that someone said it "rattled tea cups in London."

He became editor of *The Far West* newspaper. As editor he had the opportunity to turn from strictly business concerns and critically examine the broader issues of state politics. *The Far West* was published in Liberty Missouri in 1836. Copies of eight issues, each four pages long, between August and October of that year are extant.[2] The masthead of the paper read:

> By Peter H. Burnet (*sic*). Reason the Power, Truth the Weapon, and our country's good the end. Peter Rogers, proprietor.

So it appears it was a family business and the proprietor was, in fact, Burnett's father-in-law.

The first page of each edition was largely taken with, "letters to the editor" that were signed with noms-de-plume. In many cases these were in effect columnists or controversialists who appeared in

---

[2] These are digitized by Missouri Digital Heritage under: Collections: *Far West Newspaper*. http://cdm.sos.mo.gov/cdm4/browse.php?CISOROOT=%2Ffarwest. 2011/12/3.

successive issues. The remaining pages were taken with advertisements, news reports selected from many other papers, local items, curiosity items, a poetry section, and editorials all indicative of the interests and sympathies of the editor.

Many curiosity items were merely humorous. Here are examples that were of a racial character, and one reflecting his support for Andrew Jackson:

—A COLORED LAWYER. M. Pay a gentleman of color, has been recently admitted the bar of the Royal Court of Martinique to practice as an advocate. The novelty of the thing seems to have awakened considerable curiosity in this land and the court was thronged with spectators anxious to witness the ceremono (*sic*) of his accustomed oath. He was received with great kindness by his brother lawyers and on the following day he appeared as the counsil (*sic*) for several individuals, and obtained much applause for his skill and eloquence in managing his cases.

—INDIAN ELOQUENCE. In a conference between Generals Clinch and Thompson and the Seminole Chiefs, one of the latter expressed his unwillingness to leave the "land of their fathers," in the following language: "The tress (*sic*) were as his body; their branches as his limbs; the water of the land as his blood."

—THE BALTIMORE CHRONICLE STATES, "that there are upon the Whig Committee of Vigilance for Prince George's County, twenty seven influential persons who were former Jacksonians, but who now go for Harrison against Van Buren" —*Mo. Rep.*

They followed Jackson for the loaves and fishes, and being bid "go thy way and earn thy bread," they sneaked off for Harrison. Poor fellows, your portion is small.

As a member of the Liberty Blue independent militia he saw action in the Missouri Mormon War in 1838 and was at the siege of the city of Far West, where the Mormon army, including Joseph Smith, Sidney Rigdon and Lyman Wight, surrendered. Burnett discusses in his memoirs the electrifying episode of the war and his subsequent selection as part of the defense counsel for the Mormons in a civil trial. Fulfilling his father's earlier ambitions, he was admitted to the bar in

1839. He rose to be district attorney for the Clinton district—a position that carried a level of mortal hazard in those frontier days.

Unconstrained religious ideas were spreading in Missouri at that time. In addition to the Mormon upheaval, Millerites created tremendous excitement, preaching and persuading many that the end of the world would come in 1843. Campbellites were also rapidly gaining adherents. Alexander Campbell came from a Presbyterian background and was opposed to Catholicism, but Protestant sectarianism, with each sect claiming to be the true church, he found to be untenable. Before being engulfed in these ideas Burnett had pondered on the nature of the cosmos. Seeing evidence of design in the universe, he had adopted a deist position. His wife, Harriet, a devout Methodist undoubtedly influenced the development of his religious views in this period. With customary thoughtfulness, dedication, and enthusiasm, he adopted the ideas of the Campbellites.

In May 1843 Burnett's mother, now living with him and a widow of five years, died. Harriet too suffered from sickness, and as was common in those times, it was thought that a change of place and climate could be beneficial. The financial upheavals of 1837 that had resulted in the failure of some forty percent of banks nationwide continued to depress the Missouri frontier. Fueled by stories brought back by trappers, men of the frontier dreamed of leapfrogging the Rocky Mountains and seeking adventure and wealth in the Far West. Burnett also read some of the "manifest destiny" literature that suggested the natural boundaries of the United States extended to the Pacific Ocean. He was inspired to seek a better life in the Oregon Territory, and he set himself the visionary task of changing the westward flow of trappers and adventurers to include emigrant families.

He set out to organize a great train of emigrant families to distant Oregon. Making speeches, participating in ad hoc committees, and one-on-one discussions were part of his organizing activities. With Burnett as its first captain, a disparate group of families, men, women, children, wagons, and livestock; hardened military men; hardboiled mountain-men, and Catholic and Protestant missionaries experienced in the Far West, forged a decision to begin a wagon train exodus in May 1843. This expedition became known as "The Great Migration of 1843." For most of the immigrants it would be an unknown journey to a fabled location. In mid-October of that year they arrived at Fort

PROLOGUE

Walla Walla, completing an iconic migration of families. These 800 settlers would extinguish the British claims to sovereignty in Oregon, and in this way affect *global* politics.

Initially Burnett's resolute interest in Oregon was to succeed financially and pay off his debts. No doubt this attitude stemmed, in part, from the maxims instilled by his maternal grandfather on the young Peter. But the four years that he lived in Oregon proved to be remarkably transforming times for him. His first project was to build, with his partner McCarver, a new town at Linnton. However, they failed to anticipate that the shipping head of the river would be at Portland, and Linnton did not prosper immediately. He took up farming with enthusiasm and success. By April 1844 he was plowing the land to sow wheat. He also engaged in road building, a "road...barely passable with wagons," to facilitate the movement of goods to and from his farm on the Tualatin Plain.

From the 1820s the Hudson Bay Company had controlled nearly all trading operations and represented the British territorial control in the Pacific Northwest. But from February 1841 to May 1843 American trappers and settlers there struggled to form local American civic control distinct from the British claims. These efforts resulted in what was called the Organic Law and in a Legislative Committee that predated the arrival of the wagon train immigrants. In these circumstances Burnett's skills as a lawyer were badly needed. Despite some hesitation about sovereignty issues, he saw a *necessity* for local civic controls, and he was soon elected to the Legislative Committee.

In June and December 1844 legislative sessions lasting about five days each were held. Legislation was passed at a furious rate, with Burnett naturally being a major influence. These laws addressed such things as: elections, police powers, property rights, road building; and in social issues the exclusion of blacks from Oregon and a prohibition of the distillation of alcohol. He continued his work in the Provisional Government in the following years. He was appointed associate justice of the Supreme Court of Oregon by President Polk on August 14, 1848; but by the time the news of his federal appointment reached Oregon he had departed to California, and when he heard of it he declined the position.

While farming the fertile Oregon fields his mind turned to higher things, leading his religious experience to take a new turn. In the fall of 1844, when farming chores eased, he discussed religion with a close friend, a Baptist pastor. As a Campbellite, Burnett believed, of course, that the competing claims by various groups to be the true church were impossible. One of their discussions revolved around a famed debate between a Catholic, Bishop Purcell of Cincinnati, and Alexander Campbell. Burnett eagerly borrowed the pastor's copy of the debate, expecting his religious mentor to win it.[3] But in the end he concluded that Purcell had defeated Campbell in many of the exchanges. Led on by this, he says, "I procured all the works on both sides within my reach," and continued his investigation. This led him to the final step eighteen months later in June 1846 when he visited the Jesuit Father Peter De Vos in Oregon City and became a Catholic.

Gold was discovered near Sacramento, California, in January 1848. It took until August of that year before *credible* news of the bonanza arrived in Oregon. By September Burnett had organized a wagon train that he would captain on an uncharted journey to northern California. They set out, "one hundred and fifty stout, robust, energetic, sober men," in fifty wagons, early in September and arrived fifty-five days later at Longs Bar, California, without loss of life or goods. They embarked from Oregon City on the known Applegate route to Klamath Lake; from there their trailblazing created a new wagon route through prairie and uncharted mountains that Oregonians and Eastern immigrants could follow to reach the Sacramento valley and the gold fields. Along the way they rescued Peter Lassen's wagon train from destruction, as Lassen was in the process of forging that new route for immigrants to northern California. The rescue of Lassen, who was a seasoned explorer, and the difficulties of later immigrants who suffering loss of lives and goods to Indians and natural causes while following Burnett's trailblazing footsteps attests to the magnitude of his achievement and the quality of his leadership as captain of the expedition.

Burnett had come to California well prepared. Built into his wagon he had rocker equipment for placer gold mining, so that he and his nephew partnering together made good progress in working a claim at Long's Bar. However, like other astute men who joined the Gold Rush, he had his eye on making a living by professional service rather than digging.

---

[3] Alexander Campbell, *Debate on the Roman Catholic religion* (1837).

PROLOGUE

An enigmatic figure, John A. Sutter had moved to California in 1839 intent on founding New Helvetia—a *sovereign* state on the Sacramento River.[4] The finances of the outpost were precarious because of scarcity of capital and the bankruptcy of one of its backers in the Sandwich Islands (Hawaii). In 1848, Burnett teaming with Sutter's son John, used a legal maneuver to delay creditors' claims and created cash flow through the sale of real estate in a burgeoning Sacramento. As Sutter's agent, he was paid in kind, and in this way became owner of a large amount of real estate in Sacramento.

He moved easily into politics, seeing, as he had in Oregon, an urgent need for local civic control. In meetings and in letters he presented a philosophic approach making the case for statehood in California on the grounds of natural law and practical necessity. He presided at a public meeting at Sacramento, January 8, 1849, that unanimously voted for a resolution opposing slavery in California. He was also a member of the Legislative Committee of San Francisco.

The military governor, General Riley, on August 13, 1849, appointed him a judge of the Superior Tribunal, where he was elected by the other justices to be the chief justice. When the election for governor was set by the California Constitutional Convention in October he was nominated unanimously by a convention caucus to run for governor. He won the election handily in a field of distinguished competitors.

Burnett began his two year term as Governor on December 20th 1849.[5] The Mexican civic system was based on appointed mayors, or *alcaldes,* who controlled all the local functions of government. The *alcalde* was law enforcement, prosecutor, judge, and prison commander. Starting from the inherited, dysfunctional Mexican system, a state departmental administration had to be built up. He had a close relationship with his son-in-law and appointed him his secretary. The two worked closely together to review and sign the torrent of legislation that the newly founded state required. For many reasons the workload was demanding as well as hectic. California's first government had many strong-minded men with competing opinions, as is shown by the rash of fatal duels that developed among

---

[4] William Breault, *John A. Sutter in Hawaii and California 1838-1839* (Rancho Cordova, CA: Landmark Enterprises, 1998), 74.

[5] Four-year terms were inaugurated in 1864.

the legislators. Many, too, would have been personally opposed to him because of his Catholicism and his opposition to slavery. Most of the legislators were adherents of the Know Nothing Party who were fervently anti-Catholic, and elements of both the legislature and the judiciary wanted to introduce slavery notwithstanding Article 18 of the California Constitution forbidding it. Despite the gold cascading from placer mines, the fiscal aspects of statehood also proved to be very demanding. Violence in the cities and the gold fields, and between Indians and settlers continued during 1850 and was to persist for years to come.

Beyond the duties of governor Burnett had to contend with personal difficulties such as the conditions of his real estate in Sacramento. That city had been inundated with a destructive flood in January. It had been terrorized by the defiance of armed squatters in August that needed the militia to be called out before the rioting was quelled.[6] Diseases harried the city population and settlers frequently lost their lives to malaria. This state of affairs was capped by a horrendous cholera epidemic in October that killed 1000 or more. Possibly twenty percent of residents died or fled the city. Within his family he had loaned a large amount of money as capital to support his two younger brothers who were involved in a failing enterprise in Alviso. In a surprise move, Burnett offered his resignation on January 9, 1851, serving little more than one year of the two-year term.

After resigning the governorship he returned to the private practice of law. We find him also involved in *pro bono* projects. He advised Bishop Alemany in regard to Catholic property rights in the California missions, and the first bye laws for Santa Clara University can be seen in his handwriting. In April 1853 he was elected to the Sacramento City Council and served on four standing committees. In 1857 he was appointed an associate justice of the California Supreme Court.

In 1860 he published the first of four books. This book because of the title is often thought to be merely an account of his conversion to Catholicism, but it is, in fact, a unique book of apologetics.[7] One does

---

[6] See letter August 15, 1850.

[7] *The Path that led a Protestant Lawyer to the Catholic Church.* (Reissued as *The True Church: The Path that led a Protestant Lawyer to the Catholic Church* by Solas Press in 2004).

not have to share Burnett's faith to appreciate the intellectual depth and original thinking in the work. It is unique in that many of its arguments rest on commonly understood legal theory rather than on a more remote metaphysics as he shows the parallels between the "Old Church" and American jurisprudence. The work won the highest praise from the Catholic hierarchy and from Orestes Brownson who was at that time the leading American intellectual. In 1861 Burnett produced his second volume but this work bore the marks of a hasty response to the troubles of the Civil War.[8]

In a testament to his character and trustworthiness, he was chosen to head the first corporation in California in 1863—the Pacific Bank. His business activities did not leave him rich by the standards that were to prevail in the Gilded Age but he finally paid off all his debtors in Missouri. He saw his children married and two, Sallie and Armstead, die of consumption. He found time to travel to the East Coast and to visit and correspond with friends.

After his beloved Harriet's death in 1879 he retired from business and published his memoirs. He lived another fifteen years and published a book aimed at refuting the ideas of Darwinian natural selection. As an octogenarian we find him writing for and supporting the Youths' Directory of San Francisco, a charitable organization for homeless boys.

Peter Hardeman Burnett died in San Francisco April, 17 1895 and after a funeral service at St. Ignatius Church on Parker Avenue in San Francisco he was buried in the Ryland plot in the Santa Clara cemetery in the city of that name.

---

[8] *The American Theory of Government* (Out of print).

III

Interactions with Californian Indians

As a prelude to reading these letters, the accusations of xenophobia, racism and deceitful character should be looked at. Burnett worked unremittingly for the introduction of Yankee government in California and the protection it provided against anarchy, and the civil structures then offered by Confederates, Mexicans, vigilantes, and Chinese tong organizations. However, accusations against Burnett do not commonly refer to theories of government but imply a mindless, unintellectual hatred based on skin color. Thus his injustice might be supposed to be directed against "redskins," Negros, and the "yellow" races. It is worth noting that he seems to be without a trace of such bigotry on September 6, 1852, when he took pride in "Neither Jerusalem on the day of Pentecost, nor the city of Rome, in the days of the Caesars ever contained a greater variety of the human race, than does California at the present moment."[1]

The unfeasibility of a tribal society existing within an advanced nomothetic society, a society based on a system of laws and legislation, should be kept in mind when reviewing Burnett's interactions with Indians. All societies need a structure beyond the family for the protection of the common good, and the tribal civic entity necessarily bifurcates the world into *us* and *other*. This primeval impulse finds expression in language, as in the Irish *Gael* (us) and *Gaul* (other), and is sublimated only through religion and positive law. Of course, irrational impulses to war continue in advanced societies, but tribal societies treat *other* like the aptly named *dar al-harb* (house of war or chaos) of the Muslims as a proper arena for raiding. As is well known the suppression of tribal wars and raiding under *pax Romana*, worked for the flourishing of commerce and the advancement of Western society. The unfeasibility of continued tribal life comes eventually with the natural desire for the benefits of civilization.

The American experience of dealing with aboriginal peoples was preceded by the experience of the *conquistadores* and was followed by the British in Australia. In the American west there have been different approaches to coexistence with "wild" Indians. Yellow Bird,

---

[1] See his letter to Mr. Cist, September 6, 1852.

a famous Cherokee newspaper editor in early California, suggested that the Spanish missions were earlier successful in what the Federal government later sought to accomplish, to induce "[California Indians] willingly to work...and to support themselves."[2] While routine work in hunter-gatherer societies was often not the responsibility of men but of women, it is likely that Yellow Bird was aware that more than discipline and skills was required, the tribesmen needed to appreciate the economic value of labor. The endeavor of Spanish missions to integrate Indians into modern society ended in about 1833 with the secularization of the missions, and without the Indians benefiting from the vast wealth they owned in the missions.

In Oregon Dr. John McLoughlin of the Hudson Bay Company traded freely with native tribes but subjected them to a kind of *"pax* McLoughlin," which is said to have worked well with the Indian sense of justice. This effort ended after the arrival of American settlers in 1843. American solutions to coexistence invariably have rested on treaties of segregation made with the Federal Government. This way of proceeding in California in 1851 suffered from corrupt overseers and failed to assimilate tribesman into the vibrant economy. It continues to be a source of difficulty to the present, with certain tribes awarded "domestic sovereignty," and with concerns about whether the freedom and welfare of individual Indian citizens is well served.

Burnett's childhood memories would have included the stories of hostilities with Indians that must have left indelible impressions on the memories of his parents. The folklore in Nashville in the early nineteenth century would obviously include the organization of the settlement a mere generation earlier into stockades or stations for protection from Indian attack. His close connections with his mother's family, the Hardemans, would have reinforced the impact of clashes with Indians. His grandfather had participated in the Indian Wars in Tennessee and was a friend of General Andrew Jackson. Jackson as president had favored the removal of Indians from lands coveted by settlers. Burnett's uncles played a significant role in the

---

[2] Also known as John Rollins Ridge, author, editor and California newspaperman. See Christopher Burchfield "The Sweet, Sad Song of Yellow Bird, California's Confederate Cherokee" *California Territorial Quarterly*, Winter 2005, No 64: 11.

General's campaigns in the war of 1812 and against the Creek and Cherokee Indians. Later Burnett was a supporter of Jackson as President.

In the mid-nineteenth century the Far West country was a vast expanse of anarchy that was exploited by villains and Indian aggression, putting at risk any Indians and settlers inclined to peace.[3] In sparsely populated California it was impossible to prevent the settler's avariciousness for land, the murderous Indian raids and the punitive retaliatory attacks of settlers.

On April 22, 1850 Burnett signed into law "An Act for the Government and Protection of Indians." The law provided within the general mores of the times for humane and regularized interactions with the aboriginal population. Indians were not to be forced to abandon their villages or to work unwillingly. Complaints "by, for or against" Indians, as well as indentured service by adults and minor children required going before a Justice of the Peace. Given the lawless state of affairs, the policing of the provisions was largely unfeasible.[4]

Burnett as governor favored the segregation approach and was reluctant to engage in Indian fighting. In his 1851 statement to the Legislature he says:

> Among the more immediate causes that have precipitated this state of things [Indian and settler aggression], may be mentioned the neglect of the General Government to make treaties with them for their lands. We have suddenly spread ourselves over the country in every direction, and appropriated whatever portion of it we pleased to ourselves....They instinctively consider themselves a doomed race; and this idea leads to despair....This produces starvation, which knows but one law, that of gratification; and the natural result is, that these people kill the first stray animal they find.[5]

His instruction to the Major General J. H. Bean for the restoration of peace at the Gila River is noteworthy:

---

[3] See Burnett's editorial in *Far West* September 22, 1836.

[4] For an account of the escalating violence see Kimberley Johnson-Dodds, *Early California Laws and Policies Related to California Indians* (Sacramento: California State Library CRB, 2002).

[5] See appendix, EXHIBIT B, THE GOVERNOR'S MESSAGE 1851.

PROLOGUE

You will carefully instruct the officer in command of the State Militia that while it his duty to use the most determined and energetic measures, it is equally his duty to conduct his operation with prudence and with *as much humanity as may be consistent with the legitimate ends and objects of the war* (emphasis added).[6]

As governor, Burnett initiated discussions with federal agents in 1850 to settle the Indians. This gave impetus to Federal attempts in 1851 to reserve land for Indians and to reduce the temptation for raiding by providing them livestock and other goods. As noted these attempts were mainly unsuccessful.

In Burnett's reluctance for war, taken together with the respectful laudatory references to Indian characters in his writings, and with his sympathetic statement of concern for the Indian population in his report of January 1851 lies a suggestion that his resignation was in part precipitated by the brewing Mariposa War. In the comprehensive statement on Indians in his 1851 report to the Legislature, the tone of the statement undoubtedly displays Burnett's analytic approach where a political temper to his remarks might be expected. However, with a full reading of it, it would obviously be a mistake to characterize it as describing an intention, much less a policy, to exterminate the Indian population.[7] He called for disbanding military actions that he felt were not called for, and in his report to the Legislature in January 1851 he frankly defends the policy of *nonaggression* he had followed during 1850:

> Considering the number and mere predatory character of the [Indian] attacks, at so many different points along our

---

[6] See his letter to General Bean, June 1, 1850.

[7] There are many claims that Burnett had a policy of genocide. For example, see, the Huffington Post website May 19, 2011. Also, here is an example of the selective quotations that convert Burnett's description into a prescriptive statement: "California's first Governor bluntly advocated Indian genocide by declaring: 'A war of extermination will continue to be waged between the races until the Indian race becomes extinct.' " (Edward Castillo, foreword, *Exterminate Them!* eds., Clifford Trafzer and Joel Hyer, (Michigan: State University Press, 1999), x.) A slightly longer quotation would include Burnett's next sentence: "While we cannot anticipate this result but with painful regret, the inevitable destiny of the race is beyond the power or wisdom of man to avert."

whole frontier, I had determined in my own mind to leave the people of each neighborhood to protect themselves.[8]

There were, of course, some in the legislature who were unhappy with this unaggressive policy.

As noted, Burnett, on hearing in the latter part of 1850 of the brewing trouble in Mariposa, enlisted the help of the federal Indian agent, Colonel Adam Johnson, to restore peace; but the turn of events mirror well the note of despair in his January 1851 statement. In intertribal Indian wars there was an existential equilibrium in the cycle of retreat and revenge; but in any contest with the state the Indians had no chance of forcing stability—no more than the valor of the Celts in ancient times could dictate the terms of peace to Caesar and his well organized Roman legions. James Savage, a white man and a de facto Indian chief, foresaw these dangers and brought the Indian chief José Juarez to San Francisco to impress on him the suicidal nature of starting a war. But noble sentiment and the traditional logic of a human society fractured into tribelets held sway. The Indians went to war on Juarez's tragically mistaken idea that the state would not present a united front.[9]

So in regard to Indians a close reading of Burnett will find him unimpressed with the Indian way of life, "dependant on the spontaneous productions of nature," or with Indian justice "The theory of the wandering savage, to leave the kindred of the murdered victim to revenge his death, would not answer for a civilized race of men." There was no genocidal impulse, but in fact a reading will find a typical fascination with Indian culture. His strategy and sentiment appears not to have deviated radically from his attitude in Oregon when he recommended:

> The cheapest way to do this [deal with the Indian aggression in travel from Missouri to Oregon] is certainly to keep the Indians upon or near the line in peace by dealing with them fairly, and by checking the rashness of our own peoples and by cultivating a spirit of kindness and good will between the Indians and the Whites; and also by establishing Military Posts

---

[8] See appendix, EXHIBIT B, THE GOVERNOR'S MESSAGE 1851.

[9] See David A. Smith, "California and the Indian Wars: The Mariposa War." http://www.militarymuseum.org/Mariposa1.html 2007/9/12.

at suitable points along the way....It would surely be advisable for our government to pursue peaceable relations with our Indians; not only on account of the Whites, but for the sake of the Indians themselves, as well as for the honor of the country.[10]

---

[10] See Burnett's letter of October 27, 1847.

IV

Interactions with African Americans

Peter Burnett, the quintessential lawyer, was clearly, strongly influenceed by William Blackstone, the revered commentator on the laws of England. Blackstone declared that slavery is "repugnant to reason, and the principles of natural law."[1] Chattel slavery, whereby unlimited power is given to the master over the slave, has blighted human existence from prehistory to the forms of it which continue to exist at the present time.[2] It came to be associated with black racism in the eighteenth and nineteenth centuries when the predominant supply of slaves was from Africa.

With the exception of the mythologized black "Mammy" who evoked by motherly love a bonding with her white infant charges, a lack of friendships and affectionate attachments between whites and blacks was to be expected in early America. For only black persons of extraordinary ability, such as Frederick Douglass, could be expected to overcome the degradation, lack of education, training, and material goods that would permit them to operate in the give-and-take of society. Therefore those who are to be revered for their anti-slavery in the nineteenth century, the commendation of them must be based on a devotion to *justice*. And such "arm's length" devotion did not always produce the maximum in justice and fairness—after all, President Lincoln at first emancipated slaves only in the rebellious states.

Burnett, who was raised in a family that owned slaves, would as a child have viewed slavery as a natural phenomenon. This naturalness is a difficult concept to recapture. But his later discussion about his father's slave, *Uncle* Hal, and the black children as *family* show how natural it must have seemed. However, Burnett as a young man was of an independent mind and was prepared to differ from his family. Even as a teenager he thought the new Democratic Party was superior

---

[1] Sir William Blackstone (1723-1780), *Commentaries on the Laws of England*, Vol. 1, Chap. 14. Burnett freely quotes him as an authority in his writing.

[2] International Catholic Migration Commission estimated in September 2011 that 12.3 million people are enslaved worldwide, with eighty percent of the victims being female.

to his father's Whigs in politics. His emancipation from home and visit to his wealthier cousins in 1826 also whetted his appetite for understanding the broader world that was, in the Christian West, at that time influenced by the concept of freedom and the dignity of the human person.

The influence of religious principles on him in regard to slavery in his early years must remain a matter of speculation. Although his wife's family, the Hardemans and Perkins', are mentioned in the records of Mill Creek Baptist Church in Davidson County, Tennessee about the time of his birth, his own family's code appears to be based on the mere tribal dictates of his maternal grandfather. He married Harriet, a devout Methodist, in 1828, and her Christian views would be definitely influential and more religiously profound than his deist views. The influence of her Methodism seen in Burnett's enthusiasm for liquor prohibition surely extended to the Methodists' principled but wavering opposition to slavery. In 1840, in Liberty, Missouri he associated himself with the Campbellites, whose leader was sympathetic to slavery.[3] In Oregon his investigation of the true church and his conversion to Catholicism after an eighteen-month study immersed him in Christian history and thought from the Fathers of the Church to the Protestant Reformation.

Law, particularly American jurisprudence, was also clearly an influence on his thinking while in Missouri and Oregon. The Declaration of Independence enshrined the Judeo-Christian principle of the equal dignity of persons; and while the Constitution permitted continued slavery, it foreclosed the possibility that slaves could be considered *non-persons* in America.

In the nineteenth century the Western world, driven by the inhumanity of slavery, was in an ongoing process of rejecting that ancient practice. From the mid-sixteenth century the Spanish monarchy promulgated decrees against it. Agitation against slavery beginning in eighteenth century England resulted in the banning of the British African slave trade in 1807 and in an Act of Parliament to abolish slavery *in England* in 1833. Mexico banned slavery in 1823. In

---

[3] "I sympathize much more with the owners of slaves, their heirs, and successors, than with the slaves which they possess and bequeath." A. Campbell, "Our Position to American Slavery"—No. 6," *Millennial Harbinger*, Third Series, Vol. 2, No. 5 (May 1845): 233.

America of that time, the slavery controversy between North and South, that aroused high passions, had begun. Before Burnett's arrival in Oregon, the Organic Law of 1841, intent on avoiding the evils of slavery, excluded blacks from citizenship; and there was concern that the presence of freed slaves would result in a de facto slavery. Burnett at that time was opposed to slavery "as injurious to both races."

In Oregon in June 1844 he introduced a bill to the Legislative Committee, "AN ACT in regard to Slavery and Free Negroes and Mulattoes."[4] The act was designed to induce blacks not to stay in the new territory, and the penalty for not leaving within the allotted years was to be whipped every six months. The legislation was racist and anti-slavery. Burnett freely admitted the bill to be a mistake and quickly altered it at the next session before it could be implemented. However, while the revised bill removed the horrendous punishments, it retained penalties for slave owners with a view to excluding blacks from the Oregon Territory.

The American debate on slavery intensified, and Burnett pondered on it as he exercised his mind on judicial and religious questions that were a counterpart to his physical work in the Oregon farmland. After his move to California he presided at a public meeting in Sacramento on January 8, 1849, that adopted a resolution to oppose slavery "in every shape and form" in California. He boasts, "This was the first public meeting in this country that expressed its opposition to that institution."[5]

Something of the general climate surrounding his inaugural speech of 1849 can be gathered from the debates that attended the writing of the California Constitution in September of that year. In the Far West there were rumblings of Manifest Destiny doctrine but this was hardly a foundational factor among the settlers. The latter by then the overwhelming group, endured the hardship of the migration primarily for the abundant life of Oregon or the gold of California. Practical matters necessarily dominated. Their visionary outlook was that they as Americans would achieve the good life through the ideals of a sovereign, nomothetical, Christian, democratic, pluralistic,

---

[4] Burnett gives the full text in his *Recollections and Opinions of an Old Pioneer*.

[5] See his *Recollections and Opinions of an Old Pioneer*. It is reasonable to assume that the Irishman William Shannon who proposed Article 18 in the California Constitution that banned slavery, participated in this meeting.

capitalistic, state government. Elements foreign to them, Californios, Indians, Chinese, Hawaiians, Blacks, and worldwide gold seekers would not to be allowed to alter this vision.

When it came to slavery Californians might lean to the Yankee position that human dignity was offended by slavery or to the Confederate position that blacks were an inferior, naturally slave race. William Shannon on September 10, 1849 introduced the anti-slavery section and his proposal was unanimously adopted.[6] Yankees and Confederates at the Convention could both vote anti-slavery but all the framers of the Constitution, including the Californios (Mexican) delegates, were unanimous in excluding blacks from *citizenship*. Charles Botts, an attorney from Virginia, stated without contradiction:

> The States of this Union are free and sovereign. They prescribe for themselves the right of suffrage....It particularly guards you against the abuse of the powers exercised by Congress.

In his inaugural speech to the California Legislature Burnett adopted the startling position that, blacks if admitted to the state should, not be just free, but given the "full and free enjoyment of all the privileges guaranteed by the Constitution to others."[7] Here was a unique proposal, not just expressing abhorrence of slavery as many in the North had, or even a principled demand for abolition, but as governor giving a principled political demand for a post-racial society in California. These ideas were so far advanced that the national elections ten years later were to revolve about *abolition* rather than *post-racial* politics. He concludes that if the Legislature fails to give blacks equal dignity with whites and others the existence of an under-

---

[6] *Proceedings of the Convention.* http://books.google.com/.

[7] See Appendix, Inaugural Address. Also, he repeats the argument with greater force in his State of the State address of January 1851—either give blacks full citizenship or exclude them entirely. In a widely distributed book Delilah Beasley claims, "...Peter Burnet (sic), was duly inaugurated, and in his first message to the Assembly, he recommended the exclusion of 'Free Negros.' A bill was introduced in the Senate, but was indefinitely postponed." Obviously, a more accurate wording of this passage would change the thrust of her statement entirely! See Delilah Leontian Beasley, *The Negro Trail Blazers of California,* (1919) 77, 78.

privileged class would lead to strife, and they should be excluded from the State. For comparison, consider Abraham Lincoln a number of years later in 1854, who when asked whether freed blacks should be made "politically and socially our equals?" said:

> My own feelings will not admit of this, and [even] if mine would, we well know that those of the great mass of white people will not.... We can not, then, make them equals.[8]

Considering the discussions in the Constitutional Convention, of which Burnett was well aware, it can be concluded that, given the sentiment of the times, he knew that the Legislature would not vote for a post-racial society. Being aware of the general sentiment and knowing that there were pro-slavery views among the legislators, he was at the outset of his administration incurring the opposition of the majority of the Legislature. This apolitical exposition must then be taken as an example of a judicial temperament; courageously or inadvertently handing down an analysis to an unreceptive audience.

---

[8] Roy P. Basler, ed., et al., *The Collected Works of Abraham Lincoln* (New Brunswick, N. J.: Rutgers Univ. Press, 1953-1955 [eight volumes and index]), Vol. II, 255-256. From a speech delivered in Peoria, Illinois.

PROLOGUE

V

The Archy Case

In 1858 in his role as associate justice of the California Supreme Court when he handed down the ruling that returned the slave Archy Lee to his master, he paradoxically demonstrated a courageous, principled commitment, to equal dignity and rights for blacks. The background to this case involves natural law theory, federal case law and, of course, the particular circumstances in California.

Natural law being founded on the nature of man, it follows that it is not on the whole a religious concept. Its codification in the Judeo-Christian Ten Commandments states in part, "You shall not kill." Beyond the application of this to such things as the morality of war, proportional response, capital punishment, and abortion, it also demands a respect for the integrity and dignity of persons. This was the inspiration for the American Declaration of independence. But *realpolitik* intervened in the writing of the Constitution. The American Revolution was not just a social revolution, but a political revolution, and the constitution permitted the continuation of slavery. Afterward, years of coercive federal fugitive slave legislation and jurisprudence violated the sense of natural justice and freedom of conscience of those opposed to slavery, creating fear and civil disobedience. Case law protected slavery and thoroughly repudiated the moral sentiment of perhaps a half of the citizenry.

A mere ten months prior to the Archy case in California Chief Justice Roger B. Taney delivered the majority opinion of the U.S. Supreme Court in the landmark Dred Scott case. The legal reasoning of Chief Justice Taney that slaves were *mere* property was a well accepted legal position; but the extralegal considerations created a *casus belli*.

The apathy or distain for the rights of blacks, slave and freemen, at the federal level created a possibility that slavery would be nationalized and that California, with its constitutional prohibition of slavery, would be forced to accept a de facto slavery. The California Legislature under the sway of the Democratic Party of that time was hostile to the aspirations of black people. The picture of the political climate is illustrated by an event in December 1851. James Gadsden (of the Gadsden Purchase fame) wrote to Senator Thomas Green about his prior approach to Green through Isaac Holmes and his Memorial to the Legislature. The Memorial was a proposal for a slave plantation in California, he says, "A Colony which is to be the basis and stimulating influences to the permanent & future prosperity of California—Negro Slavery...."[1]

On April 15, 1852 the California Legislature passed the Fugitive Slave Law that augmented the federal act of the same name. Section 4 of the California act specified that slaves who arrived prior to the admission of California to the Union must be returned to their masters. This was undoubtedly a response to the fact that California lower courts had in many slave cases ruled the slaves to be free, since they would have arrived under Mexican law which forbade slavery.

The Perkins case brought under the 1852 act and brought before the California Supreme Court in June 1852 reveals more about the conditions in California, and has direct bearing on the Archy case. C. S. Perkins wished to remove his slaves from California under Section 4 despite their having lived as freemen for some time. Chief Justice Murray digressed from the matter at hand to say with obvious reference to Burnett's State of the State message in January 1851:

> This subject, as well as the increase of *free negro population* (emphasis added), has for some time past been a matter of serious consideration with the people of this State, in view of the pernicious consequences necessarily resulting from this class of inhabitants; so much so as to become the subject of a message from the executive of the State more than a year and a half ago.

Burnett's position in his state messages as governor, although maybe it was not shared by the Justice and others, was that the pernicious consequences flow not from the odious notions of ancestry or skin pigment but from denying black inhabitants public school education, opportunity for advancement, access to justice, and the power to vote and influence government. The pernicious consequences would be civic strife, and, Burnett suggests, would surely lead to *war*.

Associate Justice Anderson offered even more crucial statements in providing his lengthy concurring opinion in this Perkins case:

---

[1] *The Huntington Library Bulletin* No. 8, October, 1935.

PROLOGUE

> The blunder which is committed by those which consider this subject, having all their sympathies against slavery, is, that under that state of feeling, they never regard the slave as property....
>
> In connection with all these [prior] views, there is another, which, to my mind, is perfectly conclusive. Separate and apart from all others it is entitled to great weight. The 18th section of the 1st article of the [California] Constitution....There is no provision there for emancipation....The section asserts a principle, and so asserts it as to intend evidently future legislation to carry it out. *It is, as it stands, inert and inoperative*....Even as it now stands, those who do not disturb their slaves, for the purposes of reclamation, and taking them out of the country *are prevented by no law from the use of their services* (emphasis added).

This decision of the Court making Article 18 "inert and inoperative" clearly provided for slavery in California and possibly could lead to "James Gadsden type" Negro slave colonies. California was in essence no longer a "free" state.

The details of Archy Lee's various trials are very interesting with five court appearances in what some have labeled California's "Dred Scott" case. A lengthy account of this case is given by Rudolph M. Lapp. His account is of necessity somewhat speculative and has the following:

> At this time the State Supreme Court was composed of three men: Chief Justice David Terry and Associate Justices Peter H. Burnett and Stephen J. Field. Although all were Democrats, Terry and Burnett were southerners and decidedly hostile to Negro freedom, while Field was Connecticut-born with moderate anti-slavery views.[2]

---

[2] See Rudolph M. Lapp, *Archy Lee: A California Fugitive Slave Case* (Berkeley, California: Heyday Books, 2007). This kind of lightly reasoned presentation is not confined to Lapp. For example, in a forum where we would rightly expect a more accurate presentation of facts about the court we find a former associate justice of the California Supreme Court saying, "Peter Burnett, the state's first governor and *pro-slavery Democrat* (emphasis added)." It could be argued Burnett was pro-slavery as a child, but by 1850 he was clearly *anti-slavery*. See Joseph R. Grodin, "The California Supreme

A review of Field's opinions in California and when he was on the U.S. Supreme Court might have cast doubt on this "accident of birth" analysis; and as for Burnett, he was an autodidact who, led an audacious intellectual life of change. Indeed, Justice Field was later to say, "They [Terry and Burnett] were both men of vigorous minds, of generous natures and positive wills; but in all other respects *they differed as widely as it was possible for two extremes* (emphasis added)."[3]

Here, since the interest is in Burnett's landmark analysis of slavery, the full details of the case are not necessary.[4] It is enough to know that Archy was a slightly built slave boy who had a non-confrontational relationship with his young master, Charles Stovall, in California, was afraid of being returned to Mississippi, and had ill-defined ideas about freedom.[5] The case came before the Supreme Court by a writ of Chief Justice Terry, who knew Archy would be freed by a lower court. Justice Field who was traveling in the East, being absent, the case was heard by Justices Terry and Burnett.

Burnett in his opinion begins his analysis with:

> It is only our province to construe and apply the existing law. Whether that law be just or unjust, is a question for the law-maker, not for the Courts. It is not necessary therefore to inquire whether slavery is or is not contrary to the law of nature. Our individual opinions upon this question are of no

---

Court and State Constitutional Rights—Early Years," *The California Supreme Court Historical Society Newsletter,* spring/summer 2008.

[3] Stephen J. Field, *California Alcalde* (Oakland: Biobooks, 1950), 84.

[4] Archy was eventually freed by the federal judge Pen Johnson. It would seem Johnson's initial review of the case concluded that settled law was unfavorable to Archy. Then, undoubtedly influenced by Burnett's jurisprudence as well as by E. D. Baker for the defense, he made the courageous and *dangerous* decision to free him. See unsigned, undated notes, believed to be those of US Commissioner on application of Fugitive Slave Act in the case, *ca. 04/1858*. ARC Identifier 295968. Item from Record Group 21: Records of District Courts of the United States, 1685-1991

[5] See Lapp, *Archy,* page 6 "Judge Robinson took a moment [in Archy's first court appearance] to ask Archy if he really were interested in being set free. Perhaps feeling that no answer was better than a fatally wrong one, Archy remained silent." It is also clear that he was a protégé of active freedom-loving black communities in Sacramento and San Francisco.

importance in this case. The institution exists by positive law, and that positive law is paramount, and must be enforced.

This statement was a legally principled position with the added benefit of forestalling criticisms of the many who would suggest, in line with Justice Anderson's analysis, that his findings were based on "*sympathies* against slavery" (emphasis added).

He first notes the established American jurisprudence that a slave master had the right to transit a free state with his "property" on the basis of comity; *but he denies this.* Upholding the Constitutional *language* that slaves are persons; he holds that comity derives from the law of nations (natural law) and judged by that, slavery "is a mere local institution," from which it follows that it "applies only to such property as merchandise, or inanimate things, and not to slaves. The law of nations only protects such things as are generally recognized as property by civilized nations." In this Burnett did not take an ideological position of "sympathy against slavery," but displays a theoretical knowledge of law that eluded Chief Justice Taney and Justice Anderson.

He did find in Constitutional *law* a right to transit a free state with slaves, but he says, "Conceding, for the sake of argument, all that is claimed by the petitioner [the slave master], the excuse alleged does not, in our view, come within the rule."

Burnett next says "The question whether a citizen of a sister State shall be permitted to remain a reasonable time, simply as a visitor with his slaves...must depend upon the peculiar policy and situation of each State." He held, quoting precedent, that while it was theoretical possible under comity that the petitioner could do that, that in this case he having engaged in business, under this rule "his slave is entitled to freedom." Reasoning that under comity and given any participation in business, "it would be allowing a privilege to citizens of other States...what our constitution denies to our own citizens."

In denying the possibility of business activity Burnett further reaffirmed the Californian constitutional prohibition of slavery which had been declared, "inert and inoperative" in the Perkins case. Persuasively reasoning that:

> It is negative and restrictive in its terms and effect, and by its own force accomplishes the end aimed at. It operates

directly upon the state of individuals within our own territorial limits, and provides that the state of slavery should not exist therein. And when the state of slavery is abolished; then each individual is placed upon an equality, and in the contemplation of the Constitution, equally free, with all the incidents necessarily attached to the state of freedom....It was not a provision addressed solely to the legislative conscience, and dependent upon future legislation to carry it into practical effect.

Note his language, reminiscent of his addresses as governor to the Legislature, "individuals within our own territorial limits...equally free, with all the incidents necessarily attached to the state of freedom." This heralds a post-racial society, and anticipates in effect the Thirteenth and Fourteenth amendments to the federal Constitution. It directly denies *stare decisis* in contradicting Justice Anderson's "There is no provision there for emancipation."

After his groundbreaking judicial reasoning favoring the anti-slavery position, Burnett delivered a ruling contrary to his own opinion, using extralegal reasoning, and ruled that Archy should be returned to the petitioner. Why would he give an uncharacteristic, aberrant ruling that on the face of it exposed him to ridicule?

His interior motivation is not available to us but it could be supposed from the words used that he was offering inappropriate sympathy to the slave master. This is unlikely; Burnett was an exceptionally independent-minded believer in the rule of law, and had just demonstrated that independence in his precedent-setting opinion. It is also not clear what would happen if the court failed to achieve a majority and declared a mistrial. It is possible the case could revert to the lower court and Archy would be freed. Justice Terry had already used an unusual manipulation of the appellate process to bring the case before the court so there is naturally a question as to whether in the event of as mistrial he could control the procedure to bring the case to the full court where he and Justice Field would be a majority. Did the justices discuss the possible outcomes and agree how to proceed?

The weight of evidence suggests that Burnett, in sizing up the situation, wanted his precedent setting anti-slavery opinion, "equally free, with all the incidents necessarily attached to the state of freedom," to be handed down as *the opinion of the court*. The boldness and power of this strategy should not be underestimated given the Federal politics and judicial actions of the 1850's.[6] And so it was the opinion of the court, and no more Archy-type runaway slave cases or Perkins-type non-manumitted slave cases were brought before the California Supreme Court.

The Archy case can be seen as an element of Burnett's journey from being part of a slave owning family to complete rejection of slavery. In his thirties he finds slavery unjust to slave and slave owners alike and attempts to ban that institution from the new territories, albeit, initially with injustice to slaves. In his forties he proposes the possibility of a post-racial society. In his fifties, in the Archy case, he deals slavery a momentous blow. In retrospect, it appears that his finding slavery to be a "municipal institution" not worthy of comity in civilized nations is even more significant and groundbreaking than his re-enabling of Section 1, Article 18 of the California constitution.

Peter Burnett was a man of his times, but in regard to slavery he transcended them. Referring to lawyers and religion he says, "Logical minds are not prone to take a theory as true without proof; and the proofs of Christianity, though complete and conclusive to a moral certainty, yet require time and careful investigation to be able to understand them in their full and combined force.[7] This kind of philosophical enquiry caused a rejection of slavery, but it took a more intense study of religion to see the brotherhood of all men. He later expressed this:

> I believe, with St. Paul, in the unity of the human race, as expressed in the twenty-sixth verse of the seventeenth chapter

---

[6] In that period the Democratic Party was the chief proponent of slavery. Their party platform of 1860 says "[in regard] the institution of slavery...the Democratic party (sic) will abide by the decision of the Supreme Court," and "That the enactments of the State Legislatures to defeat the faithful execution of the Fugitive Slave Law, are hostile...subversive...and revolutionary." These sentiments were exactly those feared by the anti-slavery proponents to result in introducing de facto slavery into free states

[7] Peter Burnett, *Recollections and Opinions of an Old Pioneer* (Oakland: Biobooks, 1946), 86.

of Acts.[8] (And he made from one every nation of men to live on all the face of the earth...)

It would be wrong to assume that his Bible quoting was some casual, semi-political posturing. Avery Cardinal Dulles, S.J., says of him "Burnett stands in the first rank of nineteenth century American Catholic apologists." Burnett begins that apologetic work by giving strict hermeneutical rules based on his legal experience. His "inclusive reference rule" is notable, saying, "Construction should be upon the entire scripture taken and construed together, so as to give free force and effect to all the passages."[9]

---

[8] Ibid., 386.

[9] Burnett, *The True Church: The Path that Led a Protestant Lawyer to the Catholic Church* (Antioch, California: Solas Press, 2004), 3. See cover for Avery Cardinal Dulles' quote.

PROLOGUE

VI

Burnett's persona and the influx from China

The famous historian of early California, Hubert Howe Bancroft, thought Burnett too conservative. While what would constitute "too conservative" for that era may be indefinite, but as editor of a newspaper in 1836 Burnett had seen and was firmly opposed to the wild speculative state spending that contributed to the great Panic of 1837.[1] Another nineteenth century historian, William Henry Gray, was very specific in his characterization of Burnett. He says in his history of Oregon:

> Peter H. Burnett was a lawyer from Missouri, who came to Oregon to seek his fortune, as well as a religion that would pay best and give him the most influence...Mr. Burnett was unquestionably the most intelligent lawyer then in the country. He was a very ambitious man—smooth, deceitful, and insinuating in his manners.[2]

An internal analysis of Gray's work raises doubts about his accusations. In his history he claims, "The historian...by comparing the act and the result, he can arrive with almost mathematical certainty as to what the thought was that originated the act...."[3] But the reader will have doubts, since Gray is given to ascribing insular narrow mindedness to those who opposed him and describing them in vitriolic language. On the face of it, his assertion about seeking "a religion that would pay best" is untenable; it is obvious that Burnett's conversion to Catholicism could only bolster estrangement or difficulty among his compatriots at that time. It should be noted that Gray had the opportunity in the Oregon government to form his opinions over many confrontations. His choice of adjectives, "intelligent, ambitious, smooth, deceitful, insinuating," comport with a Burnett who spoke from principles rather than passion, and who compounded any discomfort in adversaries by being self-assuredly right in the legal matters considered.

---

[1] See his editorial August 11, 1836

[2] William Henry Gray, *A History of Oregon, 1792-1849: drawn from personal observation and authentic information* (published for subscribers, 1870), 374.

[3] Gray, *A History of Oregon*, 363.

Theodore Hittell, who published his encyclopedic history of California in 1885, gives a scathing indictment of Burnett. In regard to Burnett's State of the State message in 1851 he says:

> As to Chinamen, there was up to that time no proscriptive cry; and the governor therefore had nothing to say in his message against them. On the contrary the prospective commercial relations with what was called the "golden orient" and the "oldest nation in the world" rendered the Chinese residents of those early times welcome guests and their presence desirable in the civic celebrations of the day. But notwithstanding his failure to anticipate Governor Bigler in raising the cry against the Chinese, he subsequently took advantage of his autobiography to express his "unprejudiced" opinion against them as "more than a match for the white man in the struggle for existence" and to add his mite to Chinese proscription.[4]

Hittell's statement cannot be admitted as *history*, standing as it does as an unsupported opinion about interior motivations.[5]

So it is useful to review Burnett's discussion of the state of affairs in regard to Chinese to see if it supports accusations of xenophobia or of underhandedness. As already noted, by his statements to the Legislature in 1849 and 1851 that blacks could be admitted to the full franchise he was self-confident and willing to express his convictions to an unreceptive audience. It is not surprising that Burnett was at that time in his life secure in his convictions. This kind of direct, apolitical analysis can be shown again and again. For example, in his apolitical acceptance speech of the governorship in September 1849:

> She [California] has many dangers to encounter, many perils to meet. In all those countries where rich and extensive mines of the precious metals have been heretofore discovered, the people have become indolent, careless, and stupid. How far this influence may mold the character of the future population of California, time alone can determine.

---

[4] Theodore Hittel, *History of California*, 1885, Vol. IV, Book XI (San Francisco, 1898), 59.

[5] This judgment is supported by the view of Jacques Maritain who says the truth of a history depends on the "intellectual disposition" and "human richness" of the historian, but "[this] implies no subjectivism." See *On the Philosophy of History* (New York: Charles Scribner's Sons, 1957), 7-8.

PROLOGUE

Here is Burnett's assessment of the Chinese threat as he recounted it in his memoirs:

> Regarding, as I do myself, all mankind as of the same origin, these persons seem to think that the population of the globe should be left, like water, to find its own level. But this comprehensive and apparently just view is too liberal for practical statesmanship. The *practical* result would be, that the Mongolian race (the most numerous of the families of mankind) would in due time possess the country on this coast, to the ultimate exclusion of the white man....
>
> The Chinese Empire is one of vast extent, everywhere under the same compact government. It contains four hundred millions of people, about equal to one third the population of the world. These people esteem their country (and with much apparent reason) as the oldest, wealthiest, and grandest empire upon this earth. No other people are so proud of their country, or so inveterately attached to it, as are the Chinese.[6]

Undoubtedly Burnett was correct in the two points about the numerical strength of the Chinese and their attachment of to their civic structures. The population of California at the time of his inauguration was less than 150,000, and soon after, enclaves of Chinese immigrants, whom China considered to have indissoluble natural allegiance to China, were resistant to integration into the Americanized civic system. The history of California shows injustice and irrational prejudice toward the Chinese, and in the twenty-first century the Californians of Chinese extraction are highly regarded as contributors to the common good. But a reasonable person, without irrational prejudice, could well be convinced of a threat to American hegemony in California in the nineteenth century.

---

[6] Peter Burnett, *Recollections and Opinions of an Old Pioneer* (Oakland: Biobooks, 1946), 351.

VII

Conclusion

Within the confines of this short review and the primary documents given here it is possible to advance history that is all too little appreciated, to obtain an insight into life as lived in that period, and to obtain a better understanding of a historic person. The material does not deal with the grand sweep of history such as the scientific upheaval or progressivism in the arena of ideas, which were undoubtedly social forces in that era. There are the detailed descriptions of life on the trail and in Oregon, and in addition insight into the infrastructure and culture can be gleaned from a informal reading of the letters. Such insights could be about the speed and reliability of communications evident in September 4, 1850 letter, or the integration of the Californios in the new state government in the letter of June 1, 1850 that mentions Brigadier General José Maria Covarrubias.

In advocating for a state government in his letters in 1849, Burnett expressed a political philosophy that was evidently well received in California. His political pragmatism and arguments for a bedrock of moral presuppositions for law were later seen in Lincoln's national campaign. In regard to the civil war, a Western viewpoint is provided that is an addition to the abolitionist-slaveholder exchange.

Something of the development of Burnett's character and temperament can be discerned. As a child his formal education was incomplete, but this proved to be no limitation given his intellect and determination. His hard-charging character was formed in the struggle that was frontier life. Beyond the primitive struggle with the Missouri soil and weather, he faced adversity in business through immaturity in business acumen and national business cycles. In business enterprises his supported his younger brothers, assuming responsibility for their debts and capital losses. The debts he acquired he paid off many years later when living in a faroff region. When businesses failed he tried again, and simultaneously acquired a career in his true métier, law. History proved that he was resilient, magnanimous, and honest, and that he treasured family values.

He describes in his memoirs some youthful extravagant tendencies, but he had a thoughtful side that enabled him to work with the great men and scholars of his age and made him vexatious and opinionated to those with firmly held opposite views. His most profound achievement appears to have been his intellectual development. He had a vision of freedom in harmony with human nature and the Declaration of Independence, and he had the courage and confidence to defend those theories in the face of opposition.

Burnett was part of an evolving Judeo-Christian, Western mentality whose key symbol was freedom. This evolution was, as is to be expected, accompanied by undesirable events. Jacques Maritain ex-presses it well:

> Spoiled as the French Revolution may have been with Rousseauist philosophy, Jacobinism, the crimes of the Terror, and hatred and persecution of the Church, the true principles and the message of Liberty, Equality, Fraternity that is conveyed asserted themselves for their own sake...[1]

The struggle for freedom led to wars: the American Revolution, the French Revolution, and *La Giovine Italia* and associated movements that challenged despots throughout Europe. But in the eruptions of violence the ancient traditions of slavery, peonage, press gangs, and indentured service were being slowly excised from Western society. Abraham Lincoln was to expressively make the case for liberty:

> On the question of liberty, as a principle, we are not what we have been. When we were the political slaves of King George, and wanted to be free, we called the maxim that "all men are created equal" a self evident truth; but now when we have grown fat; and have lost all dread of being slaves ourselves, we have become so greedy to be *masters* that we call the same maxim "a self evident lie."[2]

---

[1] Jacques Maritain, *On the Philosophy of History* (New York: Charles Scribner's Sons, 1957), 65.

[2] Abraham Lincoln in a letter to Joshua Speed August 24, 1855. *http://showcase.netins.net/web/creative/lincoln/speeches/letters.htm.* 2011/12/26.

The most succinct description of Burnett may be that of Francis J. Lippitt, who wrote, "Judge Burnett, *a Western man of the highest character*, was nominated for Governor...."[3]

Finally, he can be an exemplar for the present in that Burnett was, not an activist, but an actor in history. Activists are noted for their inner convictions and a desire for fairness in society. But an inner gnosis is highly resistant to criticism, and the concept of fairness is exceedingly malleable. As with President Lincoln's principled call for freedom, Burnett's journey involved a rational and moral search for *justice*. When this proved to be opposed to his upbringing and popular opinion, he followed his principles with intrepidity. His life experience is a lesson in the role a rational and theoretical examination of the spiritual, legal, and political spheres has in preserving liberal democracy.

---

[3] Francis J. Lippitt, *Reminiscences of Francis J. Lippitt: Written for his family, his near family, and intimate friends* (Providence Rhode Island: The Franklin Press, 1902), 81. Emphasis added.

Part 2
Lawyer, Newspaper Editor 1830-1843

1836 August 11

THE NEXT SESSION OF THE LEGISLATURE[1]

The approaching session of the Legislature will be an important one. The subject of a State Bank, and a system of Internal Improvement will occupy no doubt a prominent share of the attention of that body. Having never been from home, and much engaged in mercantile concerns, we have never, until recently, given more than a cursory glance at the proceedings of the Rail Road Convention, which assembled in St Louis last April. The following seems to be the principal proceedings of that body:

> That measures should be adopted to construct the following Rail Roads. [Here followed a list of nine proposed railroad projects.]

It is also further:

> Resolved, that this Convention recommend to the legislature of the state, the passage of a law, authorizing a loan of not less than TEN MILLIONS of dollars, on the faith and credit of the state, to be expended under the direction of the general assembly, for the construction of works of internal improvement in the state, to be paid in installments, as the same may be needed.

The foregoing presents one of the most splendid and wide spread systems of internal improvement ever recommended in sober earnest, to the people of so new and thinly populated a state, as that of Missouri. Any individual, who will calmly and discreetly examine the proceedings of that august Convention, will inevitably conclude, in utter astonishment, that that body must have had some political object in view, and therefore could not be in earnest or else they were *a little over half crazy* at the time. They have urged the adoption of an extended system, which would be too great for the largest and most wealthy states in the Union. It is a perfect system of bribery to all the

---

[1] This is an excerpt of Peter H. Burnett's editorial in *The Far West* newspaper August 11, 1836, Digitized by the Missouri Historical Society, http://cdm.sos.mo.gov/cdm4/browse.php?CISOROOT=%2Ffarwest. 2012/1/12.

most populous counties in the state. The matter was managed with no little ingenuity in some respects, and with very little in others. The Convention was perfectly aware, that if they simply asked the Legislature for a charter to be taken by capitalists, that it would be granted; but they knew that the stock could not be sold, as no monied men would invest their funds in a rail road, the nett (*sic*) profit of which would not pay one fourth of one per cent per annum, upon the cost of construction.

The great rail roads in the Eastern States, leading from their large cities, where they receive the immense traveling custom of the great West and South, and where a heavy portion of the incalculable quantities of merchandise for the valley of the Mississippi, is transported upon said roads; are moderately profitable. But in Missouri, with a population smaller than that of the single city of Philadelphia, and with no states, and scarce any commerce west of us, could it be supposed, that all the roads recommended by the Convention, would yield enough revenue to defray the expenses of repairs &c? They would not; and of this, the Convention must have been aware, as their proceedings will show.

The St. Louis members appear to have brought forward nearly all the most prominent measures that were adopted. They were most interested. Knowing that the proposed rail roads would not be constructed by companies, in order to get over this difficulty, they proposed that the state should pledge her faith for a sum not less (it may be more) than Ten Millions of dollars.

In order to secure the adoption of this program they recommended rail roads to run through nearly every populous county in the state, so as to bribe those counties to support this wild and delusive scheme, that there might be a majority of members friendly to it in the next Legislature. If they had proposed only a single road upon which to expend the ten millions, the counties not interested, of course, would never give consent to involve the state in a debt so overwhelming,

For a state like Missouri, in its infancy, young in experience, young in population and commerce, weak in means, with only a revenue of between sixty and seventy thousand dollars per annum, to venture upon a scheme so extended, would be perfect madness. It would bring ruin upon her, and involve her in a debt, that would require ages to liquidate. We should bequeath to our posterity, a debt, under which they would groan for years, and probably centuries. Suppose the ten millions to be borrowed at six percent; (the lowest that Missouri could obtain such an immense loan for, even if she could borrow it at all,) the interest per annum would amount to the enormous sum of SIX HUNDRED THOUSAND DOLLARS!!! This would have to be raised by Taxation. If the people cannot bear the sum of $65,000 a year in taxes how would they bear the sum of $665,000 collected in tax every year? A rate of taxation sufficient to raise such a sum, would almost, if not quite depopulate the state. No man would emigrate to a state where the taxes was so exorbitant. Would the people of this state suffer their taxes to be increased nearly a thousand percent? Never. But there is still another difficulty. How would ten millions be appropriated? They would certainly be distributed proportionally among the different routes; because you never could get the members from the different sections situate near the different routes, to agree to expend the whole sum on any one road. All interested would claim a share.

After this sum should be divided between and expended upon different routes they would not more than one third or more probably one fourth completed. What is the state now to do? She must either lose the Ten millions or else borrow more and more to finish the too costly improvements, she has already undertaken. Where would the matter end? Could she borrow more? Would capitalists lend to the state a sum so much beyond her ability to pay? She could never pay even the interest on a sum of Twenty to Thirty millions, the sum which would be required to finish the wild and visionary schemes of this Rail Convention.

Such is a hasty sketch of the proceedings of this famed Convention. We have not the smallest hesitation in expressing the opinion, that this convention has been a most serious injury to the cause of internal improvements in this state. The Convention raised the spirit of improvement too high & by their chimerical and abortive schemes will let it down too low. There will be action and reaction and the public mind once excited too high, will always afterwards sink below its proper level. Some of the members have sought to ride into the Legislature upon a railroad but failed most signally. Our quondam *friend* W. F. Birch of the famed Western Monitor was the "Rail Road candidate," as the Columbia Patriot, his especial co-laborer, called him, but he had the singular misfortune to be so badly beaten, that he was ashamed to give the vote for himself in his last paper. However, he may have declined, before the election, apprehending, with instinctive horror, his dire overthrow in a political way. What a misfortune it is to stand so low in public estimation as not to be able to ride into office even upon a *hobby*.

We should sympathize with our *friend* if he had not once upon a certain occasion, when we had been unfortunate, and without any provocation, pounced upon us with the avidity of a vulture. We can now pay him up with the usual interest. We are now even.

What ever may be the course of the Legislature in regard to works of internal improvement, we are sure of one thing, that the two members of this county will oppose manfully and obstinately, the wild measures recommended by the Convention. We are well satisfied of one other matter, which is this; that the political downfall, the utter prostration, of any member or members, who will take a decided and prominent stand for those measures, will be sure and inevitable. The politician, who shall attempt to involve the state in a debt so tremendous, will be certain of political death. He will be laughed at by school boys ciphering in Simplified Addition. He will in fact and in truth be nothing but a 0 [zero] to the longest day of his existence

1836 August 18

LAND OFFICE MONEY[1]

By a late circular from the Treasury Department, nothing but gold, or silver, or Virginia Land Scrip, will be received in the land offices, after the 15th December next. The intention of this measure, is to prevent speculators from engrossing all the public lands, and converting the immense public domain into spurious paper money. The practice of receiving the bills of various banks in payments for the public lands, has heretofore given large capitalists, and grasping speculators, the power, by bank loans and bank facilities, to monopolize the larger portion of them, more especially in the South. Men of extensive wealth (the favorites of banks, and very probably their secret partners,) had nothing to do but obtain large and heavy loans, from some bank, whose paper was land office money, and which they could get on almost any time they chose, by a renewal of their notes. With the immense sums thus obtained, they were enabled at once to enter the larger portion of the valuable public lands before the honest farmer and mechanic (having no credit in a bank) could procure the lands necessary to save him a home, and a home for each of his children as they grow up. The speculator and bank favorite had the advantage of the great body of the people, not only in point of wealth but in bank facilities.

The great mass of the American people, especially in the West, consist of the farmers and mechanics, the bone and sinew of society who have no dealings with banks, and who never court their smiles. The measure under consideration, will confine the Eastern speculators to their actual capital, which is not half so great as their bank facilities, and will give the industrious and honest men of the West, time sufficient to accumulate, by their toil and labour, money enough to provide themselves homes, and a half quarter for each of their children. And more especially will it benefit the people of the upper counties when the land shall be brought into market, which lies in the new territory added to the state this session of Congress.

---

[1] This is an excerpt of Peter H. Burnett's editorial in *The Far West* newspaper August 18, 1836, Digitized by the Missouri Historical Society, http://cdm.sos.mo.gov/cdm4/browse.php?CISOROOT=%2Ffarwest. 2012/1/12.

Speculators will find it much more difficult to procure specie and bring it here, than to borrow from the banks their paper and put it into their pockets and come on without any additional trouble and expense. Our own citizens here, will be able to get the specie for all their disposable produce, as the large contracts to be filled here will give them a first rate market, and a first rate price. Independent of this the contractors with government can demand their money in specie, as nothing is a legal tender. All the specie taken in at the Lexington Land Office will be disbursed here among us, in payment of the large expenditures the government has to incur in this quarter. Besides the ordinary supplies of Fort Leavenworth, there is the immense amount of provisions required for the emigrating Indians, and the one hundred thousand dollars to be expended in opening a Military road around our frontier, and the additional regiment of Dragoons to be raised under the late law of Congress. All these expenditures, in addition to the supplies of silver we receive from Santa Fe, will throw among us every dollar necessary for all purposes, where the specie will be required.

Besides these good effects, this measure will have another one, which will terminate, we have no doubt, greatly to the benefit of the entire West. The spirit of over banking seems scarcely to know any bounds, and the banks seem to have run wild in their issues of paper. There was imminent danger that the banks, borne along upon the unprecedented and unnatural tide of prosperity, now so rapidly augmenting, would lose their prudence, and be thrown off their guard, and consequently, issue too liberally beyond their ability to redeem and the first blast of adversity would blow the great majority of them to atoms leaving the holders of their paper the innocent sufferers. This measure will effectually control this wild spirit of over issuing on the part of the banks, because their paper will be so often returned upon them for the specie for the purpose of entering lands that they will be compelled to keep their issues within the proper limits. This will give to our banks a safe, sound, and healthy action, and will check the too grasping disposition in most of them to extend their issues beyond the line of safety.

We have no doubt but some little inconvenience may be experienced by particular individuals before the altered state of things becomes familiar: but we have not the smallest doubt, that taken as a whole, it is a measure decidedly for the best interests of the

West. We would state many more reasons, but have not room or time at present

1836 September 8

The editor of the "MONITOR"[1]

The editor of the "MONITOR," in answer to our remarks, alluding to his being the Rail Road candidate, for the Legislature in his own county, states very candidly and manfully that he declined holding a poll as he apprehended defeat, but says he is not disposed to desert his principles because they are unpopular. This is manly, and what we like to see, even in an opponent. He says he may succeed at some time hereafter, possibly far in the future, when reason shall have resumed her throne. Now we do most sincerely believe that *reason, right reason,* did operate most righteously in the late election. This opinion does not arise from the most distant personal dislike to any of the aspirants. We fully agree with the editor, that it will most probably be far in the future, before his party succeeds; and we think it one of the most sensible things we have even known him to utter.

The principles he supports and sustains, must ever be unpopular with American freemen. If we understand his opinions from his editorial course, without wishing to do him, or any other individual injustice, we are clearly convinced, that he has not that confidence in the capacity of the people to govern themselves, that we entertain. He seems to doubt whether the mass of the people have the qualifications requisite to make them the proper depositories of political power. Such are our conclusions from what we have seen of his opinions as an editor.

Even if we were disposed to doubt the capacity of the mass of the people, to decide in weighty political affairs, there is one view of the subject which would induce us to give the people their way, and let them have a fair opportunity, to test the question. Monarchical writers have always insisted that the great majority of mankind were incapable of self government, and to prove the correctness of this position, they refer to the attempts heretofore made in different Republics, all of which have failed.

---

[1] This is an excerpt of Peter H. Burnett's editorial in *The Far West* newspaper September 8, 1836, Digitized by the Missouri Historical Society, http://cdm.sos.mo.gov/cdm4/browse.php?CISOROOT=%2Ffarwest. 2012/1/12.

Republican writers, on the other hand, have uniformly contended that all men by nature were equal; and, that consequently, in the nature of things; political power should be reposed in the majority of equal freemen. In reference to the failure of former experiments, they insist that they were not made under favorable circumstances, and failed for want of intelligence among the people. It is admitted on all hands that we are making that experiment under the most favorable circumstances; and if our experiment fails, the hopes of the republicans will be blasted throughout the world. We should, under such circumstances, for our own, and the good of future generations make the test experiment fairly, that the question may be settled.

Now were we a monarchist, and did we really believe that republican systems of government were unstable and insecure, we should still express no doubts on this subject, until the experiment had been fairly and fully made, and time had decided the question one way or the other.

The editor has taken a very fair, and we must say, liberal course in publishing our article upon projected Rail Roads and a State Bank. We will certainly publish his remarks in reply; and we pledge ourselves not to misrepresent him, if we know it. It is never our disposition to misrepresent any of our contemporaries. We like to discuss our points of difference in a liberal and candid manner. Had we know the facts, we should have made no allusion to the editor's race for the Legislature. Coming out so late as he did, we did not think of his declining.

1836 September 22

THE TREATY[1]

The following letter from Gen. Hughes on this subject contains the most gratifying intelligence, and we hasten to lay it before our readers without any comment as it speaks for itself.

Fort, Leavenworth,

Sept. 17th 1836.

Peter H. Burnett

Editor of the Far West:

SIR.—It is with unfeigned pleasure, after a struggle for many years, I now have it in my power to announce to you and to my fellow citizens of the "Far West," that on this day a treaty has been satisfactorily concluded with the Ioway, Sac, and Fox tribes of Indians; by which they have ceded and relinquished to the United States, all their claims to the strip of Land lying west of the State of Missouri, and North of the Missouri River. Nothing is now wanting but the confirmation of the Treaty, by the Senate of the United States, and the assent of the State of Missouri, to enable our citizens to enter, and live in peace and quietness, in this desirable country.

I shall be off in a few days, with a deputation of Indians, who desire to meet Governor Dodge in the Wisconsin territory; to hold council with him, on the subject of accession of their lands lying North of the Missouri giving room for a large state on the North of your state. If the efforts now [in the] making should be crowned with success, the Indians owning the country, will emigrate to the Southside of the Missouri River, and our citizens [will] enjoy their homes in peace, in a country, which enjoys salabrity (sic) of climate, health, mineral

---

[1] This is an excerpt of Peter H. Burnett's editorial in *The Far West* newspaper September 22, 1836, Digitized by the Missouri Historical Society, http://cdm.sos.mo.gov/cdm4/browse.php?CISOROOT=%2Ffarwest. 2012/1/12.

commercial. and agricultural advantages not to be surpassed by any section of North America.

With high respect and

with esteem. your obit. sv't

AND. [Andrew] S. HUGHES.

Nothing clearly shows the prosperous and happy conditions of our great and growing country than the view of the resources and situation of Foreign Powers. If we make a comparison between their condition and that of our own country, we shall find that we are the most free, independent and happy of all the nations of the earth. When contrasting our own institutions, and their operations, with those of other countries, it is a subject of manly and noble gratulation to reflect how superior has been their success, and. how infinitely better is our own happy condition. In the statement of the resources of the U. S. we have merely made out the items from memory, not having time to refer to any documents. As far as it goes it is substantially accurate.

UNITED STATES. —National debt *nothing*. Yearly revenue, $28,000,000. Population 15,000,000. Army in peace about 8,000 in War about 150,000. The difference in our condition may be clearly seen by contrasting the foregoing statement with the situation of Prussia, which has the same population, and nearly the same revenue as the U. States.

RESOURCES OF EUROPEAN POWERS

The Philadelphia Inquirer of Saturday contains the following statement of resources of the principal powers of Europe, which has been carefully drawn from various sources:

GREAT BRITAIN — National debt, $3,490,396,768; yearly revenue, $228,819,600; population, (say nothing of colonies,) 25,000,000; army in peace, 99,519 men; in war, 378,370; navy in peace, 610 ships; in war, 1,056.

RUSSIA —National debt, $200,000,000; yearly revenue, $52,000,000; population, (Europe and Asia,) 46,000,000; army in peace, 600,000 men; in war, 1,000,000; navy, about 140 ships, and fast increasing.

FRANCE.—National debt, $480,000,000; yearly revenue, $157,760,000; population, 34,000,000; army in peace 281;000 men; in war 320,000; navy in peace 329 ships; in war, 354.

AUSTRIA—National debt, $200,000,000; yearly revenue, $52,000,000; population, 34,500,000; army in peace, 271,404 men; in war 750,504; navy, 72 ships.

PRUSSIA —National debt, $115,840,440; yearly revenue, $30,477,000; population, 15,000,000; army in peace, 165,000 men; in war, 521,428; ships, under 20.

TURKEY—National debt, $36,000,000; yearly revenue, $11,200,000; population, (Europe and Asia,) 21,000,000; army in peace, 80,000; in war, 200,000; navy in peace, 80 ships; in war, 166.

Part 3

Explorer, Farmer, Legislator, Judge 1843–1848

1844 January

Linnton,[1]

Oregon Territory,

January 18, 1844.

James G. Bennett, Esq.

DEAR SIR

Having arrived safely in this beautiful country, and having seen, at least, its main features, I propose to give you some concise description of the same, as well as a short history of our trip. I reached the rendezvous, twenty miles from Independence, on the seventeenth of May, and found a large body of emigrants there, waiting for the company to start. On the 18th we held a meeting, and appointed a committee to see Doctor Whitman, for the purpose of obtaining information in regard to the practicability of the trip. Other committees were also appointed, and the meeting adjourned to meet again, at the Big Spring, on the 20th.

On the 20th, all the emigrants, with few exceptions, were there, as well as several from the western part of Missouri. The object of the meeting was to organize, by adopting some rules for our government. The emigrants were from various places, unacquainted with each other, and there were among them many persons emulous of distinction, and anxious to wear the honors of the company. A great difference of opinion existed as to the proper mode of organization, and many strange propositions were made. I was much amused at some of them. A fat, robust, old gentleman, who had, as he said, a great deal of "beatherlusian," whose name was McHealy, proposed that the company, by contribution, should purchase two wagons and teams for the purpose of hauling two large boats, to be taken all the way with us, that we might be able to cross the streams. A red-faced old gentleman from East Tennessee State, high up on Big Pidgeon (sic), near Kit Bullard's Mill, whose name was Dulany, generally styled "Captain," most seriously proposed that the meeting should adopt the

---

[1] Printed in *New York Herald,* Paragraph breaks added. From microfilm by the courtesy of the Green Library, Stanford University.

criminal laws of Missouri or Tennessee, for the government of the company. This proposition be supported by an able speech, and several speeches were made in reply. Some one privately suggested that we should also take along a penitentiary, if Captain Dulany's proposition should pass. These two propositions were voted for by the movers alone. A set of rules were adopted, a copy of which I send you. Capt. John Grant was employed as our pilot, and a general understanding that we should start on the 22d.

On the twenty-second of May, we commenced one of the most arduous and important trips undertaken in modern times. We traveled fifteen miles to Elm Grove, where we encamped for the night. The road and weather were most delightful, and the place of encampment most beautiful. There are only two trees in this grove—both elms—and I have learned for the first time that two trees could compose a grove. The small elm was most beautiful, in the wild and lonely prairie, and the large one had been so, but its branches had been cut off for fuel. A few small swamp dogwood bushes supplied us with fuel—and we found fuel scarcer at no place on the road than at this point.

The weather since the thirteenth of May had been fine. I have never witnessed a scene more beautiful than this. Elm Grove stands in a wide, gently undulating prairie. The moon shed her silvery light upon the white sheets of sixty wagons; a thousand herd of cattle grazed upon the surrounding plain; fifty camp fires sent up their brilliant flames, and the sound of the sweet violin was heard in the tents. All was stir and excitement

"The scene was more beautiful far to my eye,
Than If day In Its pride had arrayed it;"

The land breeze blew mild, and the azure arched sky. Looked pure as the Spirit that made it"

At the rendezvous, as well as elsewhere, we were greatly amused by the drolleries of many a curious wag. Among the rest was J. M. Ware, a most pleasant fellow, droll, original, like no one else, who had seen some of the world, and whose mimicry, dry wit, graphic descriptions, and comic songs, afforded us infinite amusement. Many of our friends, who came to visit us at the rendezvous, will never forget the pleasant evenings they spent, while witnessing the exhibitions of this comical fellow. Ware was an old bachelor, with all the eccentricity usually belonging to that sweet class of fellows. The whole camp were constantly singing his songs, and telling his tales.

Among the rest he sang

> "If I had a donkey that wouldn't go,
> Do you think I'd wallup him? no! no! no!"

And also

> "A gay young crow was sitting on an oak."

I remember well his description of George Swartz, a Dutchman, in Kentucky, who turned out a preacher. Ware said he knew him well, and was present and heard George preach his first sermon. He said George gravely arose in the pulpit, and after gazing some time around him, in a loud and commanding voice he commenced:

> Me tinks I hear my Savior say, 'Shorge, what you doin' up dar in dat bulpit?' Me say neber mind Shorge—he knows what he's 'bout—he's goin' breachin; brethren, let us bray. I tank de, 0 Lort Got, dat a few names of us have come up to worship in dy house, through the inclemency of de mud.

I will just say that Ware is here, safe and sound, and I expect to hear him repeat many of his comicalities. A few such men, on a trip like this, can beguile many a lonesome hour, and soften the asperities of the way.

The following are the rules and regulations for the government of the Oregon Emigrating Company:

Resolved, Whereas we deem it necessary for the government of all societies, either civil or military, to adopt certain rules and regulations for their government, for the purpose of keeping good order and promoting civil and military discipline. In order to insure union and safety, we deem it necessary to adopt the following rules and regulations for the government of the said company:—

Rule 1. Every male person of the age of sixteen, or upward, shall be considered a legal voter in all affairs relating to the company.

Rule 2. There shall be nine men elected by a majority of the company, who shall form a council, whose duty it shall be to settle all disputes arising between individuals, and to try and pass sentence on all persons for any act for which they may be guilty, which is subversive of good order and military discipline. They shall take especial cognizance of all sentinels and members of the guard, who may be guilty of neglect of duty, or sleeping on post. Such persons shall be tried, and sentence passed upon them at the discretion of the council. A majority of two thirds of the council shall decide all questions that may come before them, subject to the approval or disapproval of the captain. If the captain disapprove of the decision of the council, he shall state to them his reasons, when they shall again pass upon the question, and if the same decision is again made by the same majority, it shall be final.

Rule 3. There shall be a captain elected who shall have supreme military command of the company. It shall be the duty of the captain to maintain good order and strict discipline, and as far as practicable, to enforce all rules and regulations adopted by the company. Any man who shall be guilty of disobedience of orders shall be tried and sentenced at the discretion of the council, which may extend to expulsion from the company. The captain shall appoint the necessary number of duty sergeants, one of whom shall take charge of every guard, and who shall hold their offices at the pleasure of the captain.

Rule 4. There shall be an orderly sergeant elected by the company, whose duty it shall be to keep a regular roll, arranged in alphabetical order, of every person subject to guard duty in the company; and shall make out his guard details by commencing at the top of the roll and proceeding to the bottom, thus giving every man an equal tour of guard duty. He shall also give the member of every guard notice when he is detailed for duty. He shall also parade every guard, call the roll, and inspect the same at the time of mounting. He shall also visit the guard at least once every night, and see that the guard are doing strict military duty, and may at any time give them the necessary instructions respecting their duty, and shall regularly make report to the captain every morning, and be considered second in command.

Rule 5. The captain, orderly sergeant, and members of the council shall hold 'their offices at the pleasure of the company, and it shall be the duty of the council, upon the application of one third or more of the company, to order a new election for either captain, orderly sergeant, or new member or members of the council, or for all or any of them, as the case may be.

Rule 6. The election of officers shall not take place until the company meet at Kansas River.

Rule 7. No family shall be allowed to take more than three loose cattle to every male member of the family of the age of sixteen and upward.

I propose to give you a very concise description of the route, some of the most prominent objects we saw upon the way, and a statement of the distances from point to point. I will here remark, once for all, that the distances were estimated by me every evening when we encamped; and that I put them down in my journal fully as great as I think they ought to be. They are not ascertained by admeasurement, but are merely guessed at. I will now give you a table of the distances, etc., at this point, that you may the better understand what I shall afterwards relate:

	Miles
From Independence to Rendezvous	20
Rendezvous to Elm Grove	15
Elm Grove to Walkalusia	22
Same to Kansas River	31
Kansas River to Big Sandy	31
Sandy to Hurricane Branch	12
Hurricane Branch to East Fork of Blue River	20
East Fork to West Fork of Blue River	15
West Fork to where we came In sight of the Republican Fork of Blue River	41
Up Republican Fork of Blue to where we left it to cross over to Big Platte	66
Blue to Big Platte	25
Up Platte to where we saw first herd of buffalo	56
Up same to crossing on South Fork	117
Crossing to North Fork of Platte	81
Up North Fork to Cedar Grove	18
Up North Fork to Solitary Tower	18
Up North Fork to Chimney	18
Up North Fork to Scott's Bluff's	20
Up same to Fort Larimer	38

EXPLORER. FARMER. LEGISLATOR. JUDGE

Fort Larimer to Big Spring, at foot of Black Hills	8
To Keryan on North Fork	30
To crossing on North Fork	84
To Sweetwater	55
Up Sweetwater to where we first saw the eternal snows of the Rocky Mountains	60
To main dividing ridge of the Rocky Mountains	40
To first water that runs into the Pacific	2
To Little Sandy	14
To Big Sandy	14
To Green River	25
Down same	12
To Black's Fork of Green River	22
To Fort Bridger	30
To Big Muddy	20
To Bear River	37
Down Bear River to range of hills which run up to the river	57
Down Bear River to Great Saduspring	38
To Partnith first water of the Columbia	25
To Fort Hall on Snake River	58
To Partnith again	11
To Rock Creek	87
To Salmon Falls on Snake River	42
To crossing on Snake River	27
To Boiling Spring	19
To Boisé River (pronounced Boa-sle)	48
Down same to Fort Boise on Snake River	40
To Bunt River	41
Up same	25
Cross to Powder River at "Lane Pens"	18
To Grande Ronde	15
To Utilla River over Blue Mountains	43

To Doctor Whitman's	29
To Walla Walla	25

Making in all about one thousand seven hundred and twenty-six miles from Independence to Fort Walla Walla on the Columbia River. From Walla Walla to the Methodist Mission, at The Dalles, is about one hundred and twenty miles, and from The Dalles to Vancouver it is called one hundred miles, making the distance from Independence to Vancouver, by route we traveled, one thousand nine hundred and forty-six miles. I am well satisfied that the distance does not exceed two thousand miles, for the reason that ox teams could not have traveled further than we did, traveling in the manner we did.

Your friend

P. H. B.

1844 January

Linnton,[1]

Oregon Territory

1844.

James G. Bennett Esq.:—

Dear Sir—

In my former communication I gave you some account of our trip as far as Elm Grove, 15 miles from the rendezvous. On the 24th May we crossed the Walpalusia, a tributary of the Kanzas [Kansas], about twenty yards wide, clear running water, over a pebbly bed. We let our wagons down the bank (which was very steep) with ropes. There was, however, a very practicable ford, unknown to us, about 100 yards above. We saw three Potawotomie [Potawatomie] Indians, who rode fine horses, with martingales, bridals and saddles. We found very few fish in this stream.

On the 26th May we reached the Kanzas [Kansas] river, which was too high to ford; and prepared a platform, by uniting to large canoes together—and commenced crossing on the 29th. On the 27th we held a meeting, and appointed a committee of three to make arrangements for crossing the river. The committee attempted to hire Pappa's platform (a Frenchman who lived at the crossing,) but no reasonable arrangement could be made with him. Before we had finished our platform, some of the company made a private arrangement with Pappa for themselves, and commenced crossing. This produced great dissatisfaction in camp. On the 28th Pappa's platform sank, and several men, women, and children, came near being drowned, but all escaped, with the loss of some property.

---

[1] Printed in *New York Herald*, January 6 1845. Paragraph breaks added. *New York Herald* headline – Oregon Territory [Correspondance of the Herald] *Potawatomie Indians – Catholic Missionaries – Flathead Indians and Osages – Pawnee Scalps – Antelope Hunt, &c.* From microfilm by the courtesy of the Green Library, Stanford University.

As yet no organization, and no guard out. Wagons still coming in rapidly. On the 30th May, two Catholic Missionaries, to the Flat Head Indians arrived and crossed the river.

The Kanzas [Kansas] is here a wide stream, with sandy banks and bottom. I suppose it to be about a quarter mile wide at this point. The water was muddy, like that of the Missouri river. We finished crossing on the 31st May. Our encampment was on Black Warrior Creek; very uncomfortable, as our stock were constantly sticking fast in the mud upon its banks.

On the 1st June, we organized the company, by electing Peter H. Burnett commander-in-chief, and Mr. Nesmith orderly sergeant. On the 4th we crossed Big Sandy, a large creek with high banks. Last night we had a hard rain. Last evening we saw several of the Kanzas chiefs, who visited our encampment. Our usual mode of encamping was to form a hollow square with the wagons. When we organized, we had about 110 wagons and 268 men, all able to bear arms.

On the 5th we crossed the East Fork of Blue, a large creek, and a tributary of the Kanzas, and on the 6th in the evening, we crossed the West Fork of Blue, a small river, about 50 yards wide. Contrary to our expectations we found it fordable, by propping up our waggon [wagon] beds with large blocks of wood. We encamped for the night on a level prairie, dry and beautiful. In the night we had an immense thunder storm, and torrents of rain. Half the tents blew down, and nearly the whole encampment was flooded with water eight inches deep. We were in a most uncomfortable predicament next morning, and nearly all wet.

We this day met a war party of Osages and Kanzas Indians consisting of about 90 warriors. They all rode ponies, were painted, and their heads shaven, ands had one Pawnee scalp, with the ears still to it, and full of wampum. This scalp had tolerably long hair upon it, and they had divided it into some five or six different pieces some with an ear to them, and some with part of the cheek. The Kanzas and Osages are the most miserable, cowardly, and dirty Indians we saw East of the Rocky Mountains. They annoyed us greatly by their continual begging. We gave this war party bread and meat, and a calf; they said they had eaten nothing for three days. Two of this party were wounded severely, one in the shoulder and the other in another part. They had killed one Pawnee, who had wounded these two before he fell. The Kanzas Indians, however, did not steal from us, except a horse or two which were missing, but which might have escaped back to the Kanzas river.

On the 7th we removed our encampment one half mile to a place we supposed to be dry; but in the night another severe storm of rain succeeded, and again flooded half the encampment. On the 8th we travelled five miles to a grove of green elm trees, and it again rained in torrents, but our encampment was upon high ground this time. P. H. Burnett this day resigned the command of the company in consequence of ill health. On the 9th, the clouds dispersed, and we traveled five mile to find wood, where we dried our clothes. The company now separated into two parties, one under the command of Captain Jesse Applegate, and the other reorganized by electing William Martin commander. Martin's company had about 72 wagons and 175 men.

On the 10th, we met a company of four wagons from Fort Lorimer, with furs and peltries, going to Independence. They had with them several buffalo calves. As yet we saw no game of any kind, except a few straggling deer. This day Mr. Casan and others saw a corpse of an Indian in the prairie; his head had been cut off, and he badly scalped, and left to be eaten by the buzzards. This, no doubt, was the same Indian killed and scalped by the war party of Osages and Kanzas.

On the 11th, we had a fall of rain in the evening, before dark, but none in the night. On the 12th, the whole company were thrown into a state of great excitement by the news, which reached us, that Captain Grant and some others had killed a large buffalo. He was a venerable old bull, by himself, and was discovered by the hunters at about one mile distant; they run upon him with their horses, and shot him with their large horse-pistols; seven balls were fired into him before he fell. The animal was not very fat, and was tough eating. He had no doubt been left here in the spring by other buffaloes. These animals frequently come down upon the waters of Blue river (*sic*) to spend the winter among the rushes, which are abundant in the bottoms near the stream; but they return in the spring.

On the 14th June, we passed over a level plain of rich prairie land, equal to any in the world for farming purposes; but it was wild solitary prairie. On the 15th, one of the company killed an antelope— an animal not very plenty in this region, but seen occasionally for the last three or four days. June 16th, one deer and one antelope were killed, and we had a most beautiful race between an antelope ands some fleet of dogs. The animal ran down the line of wagons for about two miles, in full view, about two hundred yards from us; and as fast as he would leave one dog behind, another would come in from the wagons. Why the animal did not change course, I cannot tell, unless perhaps he was too much confused. Perhaps no animal in the world is so fleet as this beautiful creature. He will weigh about as much as a deer, has hair of much the same length and color, is formed a little like the goat, but is much more slender and neat in his form. The bucks have horns with several prongs to them, not so long as the horns of a deer, and of a black color. The bucks have black stripes, about an inch wide, running down from under each ear, and continuing under each eye toward the nose. These stripes and thin black hairs, give the animal quite a fanciful appearance. Nothing is more beautiful and graceful than the movements of this active animal. He runs very smoothly; not in irregular bounds like the deer.

Mr Linsay Applegate, who had two very fleet grey hounds with him, stated to me that he had one day witnessed a race between his best grey hound and an antelope. He said the antelope and dog were running at right angles toward each other, and the antelope did not discover the dog until the dog was within twenty feet of him. The struggle then commenced, and they ran about a quarter of a mile, each doing his utmost; but the antelope outran the dog so far, that the dog stopped still, and looked after the antelope in utter astonishment. The dog had often run upon deer and wolves with ease.

The antelope is a very wary animal, and difficult of approach. His curiosity is, however, very great; and the hunter, adapting himself to the habits of the animal, conceals himself behind a hillock of sand or other object, and putting his hat, cap, or handkerchief upon the end of his gun-stick, he raises it about two feet gently waving it back and forward. As soon as the antelope sees it, he approaches gradually nearer and nearer, making a sort of snorting noise, and alternately approaching and retreating, until he comes within reach of the hunter's trust[y] rifle. He is not very tenacious of life, and a small wound will disable him, so that he surrenders. The antelope, though exceedingly fleet, can be run down on horseback, when very fat, by continuing the chase about twenty miles.

Mr. Noland, who has been in the region of the Rocky Mountains several years, so informed me; and he also stated that wolves very frequently run them down, and that he had often fell in with the wolves and the antelope when the latter was much jaded with the race, and had then caught the antelope himself.

June 17th we encamped for the last time on Blue River. Our course since the 12th had been up the Republican Fork of Blue. Here we saw a hunting party of Pawnees who were returning from a buffalo hunt South. They had not their heads shaved like the Kanzas Indians; but their hair was cut like whitemen, and they were fine looking fellows. They had many packs of buffalo meat, which they cure by cutting it into very thin, long, and wide slices, with the grain of the meat, and the drying it in the sun. After it is dried they have a mode of pressing it between two pieces of timber, which gives it a very smooth and regular appearance. Of this meat they gave us very liberally. They amused themselves very much by imitating our driving of cattle and teams. We informed of the war party of Kanzas and Osages that we had seen, and they were very excited, and vowed to take vengeance on their enemies. They did not interrupt us, or our stock, but were very kind and friendly.

The road from Independence to this point is generally through prairie, and a most excellent road, except the fords upon the streams, which are miry and difficult to cross. The Kanzas country, as it may be called, is 19/20ths prairie, generally fertile, but destitute of timber, except upon the streams. This timber is elm, low bur oak, and small swamp ash, along the margin of the streams. I saw only a very few places where good farms could be made; for want of timber. This whole country has very little game of any kind, except a very few wild deer and antelope. We saw no squirrels on Blue, and very few birds, except a small species of snipe. I remember a wild cat, killed by some one in the company, that was a mere skeleton, from starvation, no doubt. But few fish were found in the stream.

Your Friend

P.H.B.

1844 January

Linnton,[1]

Oregon Territory

1844

James G. Bennett, Esq.:—

Dear Sir—

In my letter of the 26th inst., I continued my account of our trip to our last encampment upon the waters of the Blue. On the 18th day of June we crossed the main dividing ridge between the waters of the Kanzas (*sic*) and the Great Platte. We travelled twenty five miles over the finest road imaginable, and our eyes first beheld the wide and beautiful valley of the Great Platte just as the sun (*sic*) was going down behind the bleak sand hills. We encamped in the bottom, about two miles from the river, without fuel. Next morning we started, without any breakfast, and travelled a few miles, where we found willows for fuel, and where we took a hearty meal.

We struck the river near the head of Grand Island which is seventy-five miles long, covered with timber, and several miles wide, varying greatly, in places, as to width; but what was strange, there was not a solitary tree on the south side of the river where we were. The river above the island, and as far as the Forks, is generally about 2 miles wide. Perhaps this is one of the most remarkable rivers in the world. Like the Nile, it runs hundreds of miles through a sandy desert. The valley of the stream is from 15 to 20 miles wide, a smooth level plain, and the river generally runs in the middle of it, from west to east. The course of the stream is more uniform than any I have ever seen. It scarcely ever makes a bend. The Platte river (*sic*) was very high until after we had passed Fort Larimer. This river has low sandy banks, with sandy bottom, and the water muddy, like that of the

---

[1] Printed in the *New York Weekly Herald* January 18th 1845. *New York Herald* headlines — Oregon Territory [Correspondence of the Herald]. *The Great Platte River – White Wolves – Buffalo Hunting and Eating.* Paragraph breaks were added. From microfilm by the courtesy of the Green Library, Stanford University.

Missouri. The current is rapid, and the river being very wide, is very shallow, and easily forded, except in high water. It is full of most beautiful islands of all sizes, covered with beautiful trees, contrasting finely with the wild prairie plains and bold sand hill on each side of the river. The plain on each side of the river extends out to the sand hills, which is about three miles through them, when you ascend up a wide prairie plain of almost interminable extent.

Upon this plain, and sometimes in the sand hills, we found the buffalo, and numbers of white wolves. In the plains, near the river, we generally found the antelope. When the season is wet, as was the case this season, the buffalo resort to the plain beyond the sand hills, where they find water in ponds. As summer advances, and the ponds dry up, they approach the river, and are found in the plain near it.

You have, perhaps, often heard of buffalo paths. As you go from the river out to the wide plain, beyond the sand hills, through which you must pass, you will find vallies (sic) among the hills leading out toward this plain. These vallies (sic) are covered with grass, and the buffalo have made numerous paths, not only in these vallies (sic), but over all the hills, where they could pass at all, (and they can pass almost anywhere,) leading from this wide plain to the river, where they resort for water in the dry season. These paths are very narrow, and are sunk in the ground six or eight inches deep. In travelling up the Platte, almost every thirty yards we had to cross a path, which was about all the obstructions we met while travelling up this gently inclined plain. While hunting, there is no danger of being lost, for you can find a buffalo path anywhere, and they always lead the nearest route to the river.

All the plains are covered with grass but the plain upon the river has not only the greatest variety, but the most rich and luxuriant grass. The greatest general scarcity of wood we found on the Platte, before we reached Fort Larimer. We sometimes found bunches of dry willows, often Indian wigwams made of willow; but the way in which we generally procured our fuel, was to pick up the pieces of drift wood during the day, and at night we would have plenty. It requires very little fuel. It is necessary to dig a narrow ditch, about eight inches wide, one foot deep, and two or three feet long. This confines the heat, and prevents the wind from scattering the fire.

On the 22d day of June we saw the first band of buffaloes, which contained about fifty of all ages and sizes. Out of this band two were killed. They were found in the plain close to the river and were pursued on horseback. Perhaps no sport in the world is so exciting as a buffalo hunt. The fox chase sinks into insignificance when compared to it.

The mode of hunting this noble animal is very simple. They are generally found upon the wide plain beyond the sand hills , as I before stated, and you will almost always find their grazing near the head of some hollow leading up near them. When you approach him, you must let the wind blow from him to you; because if you scent him, you will hardly run off, but if he scents you, he is certain to scamper. The sight of the buffalo is very dull, but their sense of smell is acute. I one day saw a band of about one hundred buffaloes on the opposite side of the river from us, and about two mile off, running parallel with the line of the wagons, up the river. When they came directly opposite to us, so as to strike the stream of wind which blew directly from us across the river, they turned suddenly off at right angles, and increased their speed greatly. They had evidently scented us.

If you have the wind of them, you can approach within a very short distance, near enough to kill them readily with a rifle. When you fire, if you remain still, and do not show yourself, the buffalo will perhaps bring a bound, and then stop, and remain until you have fired several times. If he is wounded he will he will lie down. If several guns are fired in quick succession it alarms the band and they all move off in a brisk trot; but if you load and fire slowly, you may often kill several before the balance leave. I have seen three or four lying within ten yards of each other. When you have fired as often as you can , and the buffaloes have retired beyond the range of your balls, you return down the hollow to your horses, and having mounted, you approach as near as possible before you show yourself to the animal; and when he sees you, your horse ought to be at the very top of his speed, so as to get near him before he goes under full speed You may dash at a band of buffaloes not more than one hundred yards off, and they will stand and gaze at you before they start; but when one puts himself in motion, all the rest move instantly, and those lying down will not be very far behind the others; as they rise running. Although they seem to run awkwardly, yet they step away rapidly, and if you lose much time, you will have a hard run to overtake them. The better plan is to put your horse to the top speed at once. This enables you to press upon the buffaloe (*sic*) at the first of the race, and when you approach within fifty or sixty yards of them, you will find they can let out a few more links; and if a bull is wounded, even very slightly, the moment you press hard upon him, he will turn short around, curl his tail over his back, bow his neck, and face you for a fight. At this time you had as well keep at a convenient distance. If you keep off about fifty yards, he will stand, and you may load and fire several times; but you had better not fire at his head, for you will not hurt him much if you hit him, for the ball will never penetrate through the skull bone. Whenever you bring one to bay, if the country is not too broken, and your horse is good, there is no danger of his escape, as you may shoot as often as you please; and whenever you give the animal a deadly shot, he will kick as if kicking at some object that attacks him.

The buffalo, when excited, is very hard to kill, and you may put several balls through his heart, and he will then live, sometimes, for hours. The best place to shoot them is behind the shoulder at the bulge of the ribs, and just below the back bone, so as to pass through the thick part of the lungs. This is the most deadly of all shots; and when you see the animal cough up blood, it is unnecessary to shoot him any more. When you shoot them through the lungs, the blood smothers them immediately. The lungs of the buffalo are very large, and easily hit by any sort of marksman. If you pursue a buffalo, not wounded, you may run up by his side, and shoot off your horse. The animal becomes tired, after running at top speed for two or three miles, and will then run at a slow gallop. The buffalo is a most noble animal—very formidable in his appearance—and, in the summer, has a very short, soft coat of fine wool over his body, from behind his shoulders to his tail. His neck and head are covered with a thick mass of long black wool, almost concealing his short thick horns, (the points of which just peep out,) and his small eye. This animal has a great deal of bold daring, and it is difficult to turn him from his course.

On the 27th of June we had stopped our wagons, about one half mile from the river, to spend the noon, and rest our teams. While there, we discovered seven large buffalo bulls, slowly moving up the river on the opposite side; and when they were about opposite to us, they plunged into the river, and swam across toward us, in the face of wagons, teams, cattle, horses, men and all. Every man shouldered his gun, and some went up, and some went down the river, so as to form a complete semi-circle. We were all certain that the buffaloe (*sic*) would turn back, and recross the river; but on they came, merely turning their course a little around the wagons. You never heard such a bombardment in all your life. Not a buffalo escaped unhurt; and three or four were killed within a short distance. The buffalo, being a very large object, can be seen at a great distance.

Perhaps the flesh of no animal is more delicious than that of a young buffalo cow, in good order. You may eat as much as you please, and it will not oppress you. The flesh of the antelope is fine eating, equal to good venison, but more juicy. I remember while we were upon the Sweetwater, that we remained in one place a day or two; and that one evening I came in from hunting, very hungry. Captain Gant had killed a very fat buffalo cow, and had made me a present of some choice pieces. It was after dinner, and Mrs. B. had six large slices of this meat cooked for me. I supposed I could eat three of them, as I thought they would be sufficient for anyone; but when I had eaten them, I felt a strong inclination to the fourth, and so I eat them all. About two hours afterwards, supper came on, and we had more of this fine meat. Dr. Long rook supper with me, and something was said about Oregon. The Doctor remarked, that he feared Oregon was like the buffalo meat, overrated. Said I, "Doctor, I have always thought as you do in regard to buffalo meat until this day, and now I think it has always been underrated." I continued eating until I was ashamed, and left super hungry. I then went to Capt. Gant's tent; and there he had some buffalo tongue cooked nicely, and insisted I should eat a piece. I sat down and eat (sic) of the buffalo tongue until I was ashamed, and then went to bed hungry. From this you may infer, that I was a gormandizer; but if I can judge impartially, in my own case, I assure you, I was not more so than most persons on the road.

Your friend,

P.H.B.

1844 January

Linnton,[1]

1844

James G. Bennett, Esq:—

Dear Sir:—

The proper outfit for emigrants is a matter of very great importance, as upon it depends the ease of the journey. As little as we knew about the matter, we were well enough prepared to get here, all safe, and without much suffering on the road. I would even be most willing to travel the same road twice over again, had I the means to purchase cattle in the States; and Mrs. B. (who performed as much labor on the road as any other woman,) would most gladly undertake the trip again.

There is a good deal of labor to perform on the road, but the weather is so dry and the air so pure and pleasant, and your appetite so good, that the labor becomes easy. I had more pleasure in eating on this trip than I ever did in the same time before, which would have been greater had it not been for the eternal apprehension of difficulties ahead. Whether we were to leave our wagons, or whether we were to be out of provisions, was all uncertain, and kept us in a state of painful suspense. This state of uncertainty cannot exist again, as the way is broken and conclusively shown to be practicable. The sedge, which was a great impediment to us, we broke down completely, and left behind us a good wagon road, smooth and easy. Those who come after us will be better prepared, and they will have no apprehension about a scarcity of provisions. There is not the slightest danger of starvation, and not the least danger of suffering, if even ordinary care is taken, Emigrants may now come, knowing that the property they start with they can bring clear through; and when

---

[1] Printed January 6, 1845. *New York Herald* headline —*Outfit for Emigrants—Value of Cattle in Oregon—Wagons—The proper time for Emigrants to start—Mode of Travel—Buffaloes, etc.* From microfilm by the courtesy of the Green Library, Stanford University.

they reach here it will be worth about twice, and some of it (all their cattle) four times as much as it was when they left the States.

There is no danger of suffering for water, as you will find it every evening, and always good, except perhaps at one or two places—not more; and by filling a four gallon keg every morning, you have it convenient all day. Fuel on the way is scarce at some points, but we never suffered for want of fuel. You travel up or down streams nearly all the way, upon which you will find dry willows, which make an excellent fire, and where you find no willows the sedge answers all purposes. Nothing burns more brilliantly than the sedge; even the green seems to burn almost as readily as the dry, and it catches as quick as dry shavings, but it does not make as good coal to cook with as the willows. The wagons for this trip should be two horse wagons, plain yankee beds, the running gear made of good materials, and fine workmanship, with falling tongues; and all in a state of good repair. A few extra iron bolts, linchpins, skanes, paint bands for the axel, one cold chisel, a few pounds of wrought nails, assorted, several papers of cut tacks, and some hoop iron, and a punch for making holes in the hoop iron, a few chisels, handsaw, drawing knife, axes, and tools generally, it would be well to bring, especially augers, as they may be needed on the way for repairing. All light tools that a man has, that do not weight too much, he ought to bring. Falling tongues are greatly superior to others, though both will do. You frequently pass across hollows, that have very steep, but short banks, where falling tongues are preferable, and there are no trees on the way to break them. The wagon sheets should be double, and not painted, as that makes them break. The wagon bows should be well make and strong, and it is best to have side boards, and have the upper edge of the wagon body beveled outwards, so that the water running down the wagon sheet, when it strikes the body, may run down on the outside. And it is well to have the bottom of the bed beveled in the same way, that the water may not run inside the wagon. Having your wagons well prepared, they are as secure, almost, as a house. Tents and wagon sheets are best made of heavy brown cotton drilling, and will last well all the way. They should be well fastened down.

When you reach the mountains, if your wagons are not well made of seasoned timbers, the tires become loose. This is very easily repaired by taking the hoop iron, taking the nails out the tire and driving the hoop iron under the tire and between it and the felloes; the tire you punch, and make holes through the hoop iron and drive in your nails, and all will be tight. Another mode of tightening the tire, which answers very well, is to drive pine wedges crosswise under it, which holds it tight. If your wagons are even ordinarily good the tire will never become loose, and you will not perhaps have to repair any on the whole trip. Any wagon that will perform a journey from Kentucky to Missouri, will stand the trip well. There many wagons in Oregon, brought through last year, that are both old and very ordinary. It is much easier to repair a wagon on the way than you would suppose. Beware of heavy wagons, as they break down your teams for no purpose, and you will not need them. Light wagons will carry all you want, as there is nothing to break them down, no logs, no stumps, no rock, until you get more than half way, when your load is so much reduced, that there is then no danger. You see no stumps on the road until you get to Burnt river, and very few there, and no rock until you get into the Black Hills, and only there for a short distance, and not bad, and then you will see none until you reach the Great Soda Spring, on Bear river—at least, none of any consequence. If an individual should have several wagons, some good and some ordinary, he might start with all of them; and his ordinary wagons will go to the mountains, where his load will be so reduced that his other wagons will do. It is not necessary to bring along an extra axle-tree, as you will rarely break one. A few pieces of well seasoned hickory, for the wedges and the like, you ought to bring.

Teams.—The best teams for this trip are ox teams. Let the oxen be from three to five years old, well set, and compactly built; just such oxen as are best for use at home. They should not be too heavy, as their feet will not bear the trip so well. But oxen six, seven and eight years old, some of them very large, stood the trip last year very well, but not so well in general as the younger and lighter ones. Young cows make just as good a team as any. It is the travel and not the pulling that tires your team, until after you reach Fort Hall. If you have cows for a team it requires more of them in bad roads, but they stand the trip equally well, if not better, than oxen. We fully tested the ox and mule teams, and we found the ox teams greatly superior. One ox will pull as much as two mules, and, in mud, as much as four. They are more easily managed, are not so subject to be lost or broken down on the way, cost less at the start, and are worth about four times as much here. The ox is a most noble animal, patient, thrifty, durable, gentle, and easily driven, and does not run off. Those who come to this country will be in love with their oxen by the time they reach here. The ox will plunge through mud, swim over streams, dive into thickets, and climb mountains to get at the grass, and he will eat almost anything. Willows they eat with great greediness on the way; and it is next to impossible to drown an ox.

I would advise all emigrants to bring all the cattle they can procure, to this country, and all their horses, as they will with proper care, stand the trip well. We found a good horse to stand the trip as well as a mule. Horses need shoeing, but oxen do not. I had ox shoes made, and so did many others, but it was money thrown away. If a man had five hundred dollars, and would invest it in young heifers in the States and drive them here, they would here be worth at least five thousand dollars and by engaging in stock raising, he could make an independent fortune. Milch cows on the road are exceedingly useful, as they give an abundance of milk all the way, though less towards the close of it. By making what is called thickened milk on the way, a great saving of flour is effected, and it is a most rich and delicious food, especially for children. We found that yearling calves and even sucking calves, stood the trip very well, but the sucking calves had all the milk.

Provisions—

160 pounds of flour and 40 pounds bacon to each person. Besides this, as much dried fruit, rice, corn meal, parched corn meal, and raw corn, peas, sugar, tea, coffee, and such like articles as you can well bring. Flour will keep sweet the whole trip, corn meal to the mountains, and parched corn meal all the way. The flour and meal ought to be put in sacks or light barrels; and what they call shorts are just as good as the finest flour, and will perhaps keep better; but I do not remember of any flour being spoiled on the way. The parched corn meal is most excellent to make a soup. Dried fruit is most excellent. A few beef cattle to kill on the way, or fat calves, are very useful, as you need fresh meat. Peas are most excellent. The loading should consist mostly of provisions. Emigrants should not burthen themselves with furniture, or many beds; and a few light trunks, or very light boxes might be brought to pack clothes in. Trunks are best, but they should be light. All heavy articles should be left, except a few cooking vessels, one shovel, and a pair of pot hooks. Clothes enough to last a year, and several pair of strong heavy shoes to each person, it will be well to bring. If you are heavily loaded, let the quantity of sugar and coffee be small, as milk is preferable, and does not have to

be hauled. You should have a water keg, and a tin canister, made like a powder canister, to hold your milk in; a few tin cups, tin plates, tin saucers, and butcher knives; and there should be a small grindstone in company, as the tools become dull on the way. Many other articles may be useful. Rifles and shot guns, pistols, powder, lead, and shot, I need hardly say, are useful, and some of them necessary on the road, and sell well here. A rifle that would cost twenty dollars in the States, is worth fifty dollars here, and shot guns in proportion. The road will be found, upon the whole, the best road in the world, considering its length. On the Platte, the only inconvenience arising from the road is the propensity to sleep in the day time. The air is so pleasant, and the road so smooth, that I have known many a teamster to go fast asleep in his wagon, and his team stop still in the road. The usual plan was for the wagons behind to drive around him, and leave him until he waked up, when he would come driving up, looking rather sheepish.

Emigrants should start as early as possible in ordinary seasons; by first of May at farthest; even as early as first of April would do. For those emigrants coming from the Platte country, it is thought that they had better cross the Missouri river at McPherson's Ferry, in Hatt county, and take up the ridge between Platte and Kanzas rivers; but I cannot determine that question. Companies of from forty to fifty wagons are large enough. Americans are prone to differ in opinion, and large companies become unwieldy, and the stock become more troublesome. In driving stock to this country, about one in ten is lost; not more. Having started, the best way to save the teams is to drive a reasonable distance every day, and stop about an hour before sundown. This gives time for arranging the camp, and for the teams to rest and eat before it is dark. About eight hours' drive in long days—resting one hour at noon—I think, is enough. Never drive irregularly, if you can avoid it. On Platte river, Bear river, and Boise river, and in many other places, you can camp at any point you please; but at other places on the way, you will be compelled to drive hard some days, to get to water and range. When you reach the country of buffalo, never stop your wagons to hunt, as you will eat up more provisions than you will save. It is true, you can kill buffalo, but they are always far from camp, and the weather is too warm to save much of it. When you reach the country of game, those, who have good horses can keep the company in fresh meat. If an individual wishes to have great amusement hunting the buffalo, he had better have an extra horse, and not use him until he reaches the buffalo region. Buffalo hunting is very hard upon horses; and emigrants had better be cautious how they unnecessarily break down their horses. A prudent care should be taken of horses, teams, and provisions, from the start. Nothing should be wasted or thrown away that can be eaten.

If a prudent course is taken, the trip can be made, in ordinary seasons, in four months. It took us longer; but we lost a great deal of time on the road, and had the way to break. Other routes than the one traveled by us, and better routes, may be found. Captain Gant, our pilot, was decidedly of the opinion that to keep up the south Fork of Platte, and cross it just above a stream running into it called the Kashlapood, and thence up the latter stream, passing between the Black hills, on your right, and peaks of the Rocky mountains of your left, and striking our route at Green river, would be a better and nearer route—more plentifully supplied with game than the one we came. He had traveled both routes, and brought us the route he did, because he had been informed that large bands of the Sioux Indians were hunting upon the southern route.

The trip to Oregon is not a costly or expensive one. An individual can more here as cheap, of not cheaper, than he can from Tennessee or Kentucky to Missouri. All the property you start with you cam bring through; and it is worth thribble [triple] as much as when you started. There is no country in the world where the wants of man can be so easily supplied, upon such easy terms, as this; and none where the beauties of nature are displayed upon a grander scale.

Your friend PHB

1844 January

Linnton,[1]

Oregon Territory

1844

The fisheries of this country are immense. Foremost among all the fish of this, or any other country is the salmon. Of the numbers of this fish taken annually, in the Columbia river (sic) and its tributaries, it would be impossible to state. They have been estimated at ten thousand barrels annually, which I think is not too large. The salmon is a beautiful fish, long, round and plump, weighing generally about twenty pounds, very fat, and yet no food of any kind is ever found in its stomach. What they eat no one can tell. Sir Humphrey Davy supposed that the gastric juice of the salmon was so powerful as instantly to dissolve all substances entering the stomach.

The salmon in this country is never caught with a hook; but they are sometimes taken by the Indians with small scoop nets, and generally with a sort of spear, of very peculiar construction, which I will describe. They take a pole, made of some hardwood, say ten feet long and one inch in diameter, gradually sharpened to a point at one end. They then cut off a piece from the sharp prong of a buck's horn, about four inches long, and hollow out the large end of this piece so that it fits on the end of the pole. About the middle of the black horn they make a hole, through which they put a small cord or leather string, which they fasten to the pole about two feet from the lower end. When they spear a fish, the spear passes through the body, the buck-horn comes off the pole, and the pole pulls out of the hole made by the spear, but the buck-horn remains on the opposite side of the fish, and he is held fact by the string, from which it is impossible to escape.

All the salmon caught here are taken by the Indians, and sold to the whites at about ten cents each, and frequently for less. One Indian

---

[1] *The New York Herald*, December 28, 1844 Vol, X No 399 —Whole No. 3909. Headline – Letters from the Oregon Territory (Correspondence of the Herald). From microfilm by the courtesy of the Green Library, Stanford University.

will take about twenty per day upon average. The salmon taken at different points vary greatly in kind and quality, and it is only at particular places that they can be taken. The fatest (*sic*) and best salmon are caught at the mouth of the Columbia; the next best are those taken in the Columbia, a few miles below Vancouver, at the Cascades, and at the Dalles. Those taken at the Wallamette [Willamette] Falls are smaller and inferior and are said to be of a different kind. What is singular, this fish cannot be taken in any considerable numbers with large seines. This fish is too shy and too active to be thus taken. I believe no white man has yet succeeded in taking them with a jig. The salmon make their appearance in the vicinity of Vancouver, first in Klackmas. The best salmon are taken in June. The sturgeon is a very large fish, caught with a hook and line, and is good eating. They are taken in the Wallamette [Willamette], below the Falls, and in the Columbia at all points, and in Soake river (*sic*) as high as Fort Baise.

NAVIGATION—

As I have before stated, the navigation of the Columbia is good to the Ialles [Dalles],with the exception of the Cascades, The river near the ocean is very wide, forming bays, and is subject to high winds, which render the navigation unsafe for small craft. The difficulties at the mouth of the river will rapidly diminish as business increases, and they have regular pilots and steam tow boats. Ships pass up the Wallamette [Willamette] some five miles above Linnton, where there is a bar; but small ships go up higher, and to within seven or eight miles of the Falls. Above the Falls, the Wallamette [Willamette] is navigable for steam boats about fifty miles. Tom Hill River is navigable for canoes and keelboats up to the forks, the distance I can not say. The navigation of this, the first section, is much better than that of the second section.

WATER POWER.—The water power of this country is unequaled, and is found distributed throughout this section. The water power at the falls of the Wallamette can not be surpassed in the world. Any quantity of machinery can be put. in motion; but the good water power is not confined to the Wallamette Falls. Everywhere on the Columbia and Wallamette rivers there are mill sites as good, but not so large as the falls. Most of the mill sites in this country are overshots; but we have not only the finest water power, but we have the (best? finest timber***).

TIMBER.—The timber of this section of Oregon constitutes one main source of its wealth. It is found in inexhaustible quantities on the Columbia and on the Wallamette, just where the water power is at hand to cut it up, and where ships can take it on board. The principal timber of this section is the fir, white cedar, white oak, and black ash. There three kinds of fir,—the white, yellow, and red, all of them fine timber for planks, shingles, boards, and rails. The white fir makes the best shingles. The fir is a species of the pine, grows very tall and straight, and stands very thick upon the ground. Thick as they stand upon the ground, when you cut one it never lodges, for the reason this timber never forks, and the limbs are too small to stop a falling tree. You can find them in the vicinity of Linnton, from eight feet in diameter to small saplings; and the tallest of them will measure about two hundred and twenty-five feet. In the Cascade Mountains, and near the mouth of the Columbia River, they rise to the height of three hundred feet. The fir splits exceedingly well, and makes the finest boards of any timber I have ever seen. I cut one tree from which I sawed twenty-four cuts of three-foot boards, and there are plenty of such trees all around me, yet untouched. The white cedar is a very fine timber, nearly if not quite equal to the red cedar in the States.

The wild animals of this the first section of Oregon, are the black bear, black-tailed deer, raccoon, panther, polecat, rabbit, wolf, beaver, and a few others. Deer and wolves are plenty. We have no buffaloes, antelopes, or prairie chickens here, but in the second section prairie chickens are plenty. As for birds, we have the bluejay, larger than the jay of the States, and deep blue. We have also the nut-brown wren, a most beautiful and gentle little bird. very little larger than the humming bird. Also, a species of bird which resembles the robin in form, color, and size. Also, a bird that sings the livelong night; but although I have heard them often, I have never seen one. The bald eagle, so well described by Wilson, is here found all along the rivers, but he was here to catch his own game, as there are no fish-hawks to do it for him. The eagle here feeds principally upon the dead salmon that float down the rivers, for you are aware, perhaps, that out of the myriads of salmon that ascend the rivers of Oregon, not one ever finds the way back to the ocean. They are never found swimming down stream, but their last effort is to ascend. The eagle also feeds upon wild ducks, which he catches as follows: He darts at the duck while in the water, and the duck dives, but as soon as he rises to the surface, the eagle, having turned himself, strikes at the duck again and the duck again dives. This manoeuvre the eagle continues until the duck becomes tired, when the eagle nabs him just as he rises to the top of the water. The duck seems to be afraid to attempt escape upon the wing. We have also pheasants very abundant, and they are most excellent eating. Like old Ireland itself, there are no poisonous reptiles or insects in this section of Oregon. The only snake is the small harmless garter snake, and there are no flies to annoy the cattle.

MOUNTAINS.—We have the most beautiful scenery in North America—the largest ocean, the purest and most beautiful streams, and loftiest and most beautiful trees. The several peaks of the Cascade range of mountains are grand and imposing objects. From Vancouver you have a fair and full view of Mount Hood, perhaps the tallest peak of the Cascades, and which rises nearly sixteen thousand feet above the level of the Pacific, and ten thousand feet above the surrounding mountains. This lofty pile rises up by itself, and is in form of a regular cone, covered with perpetual snow. This is the only peak you can see from Vancouver, as the view is obscured by the tall fir timber. At the mouth of the Wallamette, as you enter the Columbia, you have a view of both Mount Hood and Mount St. Helena. From Linnton you have a very fair and full view of Mount St. Helena, about fifty miles distant; but it looks as if it was within reach. This peak is very smooth, and in the form of a regular cone, and nearly, if not quite, as tall as Mount Hood, and also covered with perpetual snow. This mountain is now a burning volcano. It commenced about a year since. The crater is on the side of the mountain, about two thirds of the distance from its base. This peak, like Mount Hood, stands far off and alone, in its solitary grandeur, rising far, far above all surrounding objects. On the sixteenth of February, 1844, being a beautiful and clear day, the mountain burned most magnificently. The dense masses of smoke rose up in one immense column, covering the whole crest of the mountain in clouds. Like other volcanoes, it burns at Intervals. This mountain is second to but one volcanic mountain in the world, Cotopaxi, in South America. On the side of the mountain, near its top, is a large black object, amidst the pure white snow around it. This is supposed to be the mouth of a large cavern. From Indian accounts this mountain emitted a volume of burning lava about the time it first commenced burning. An Indian came to Vancouver with his foot and leg badly burnt, who stated that he was on the side of the mountain hunting deer, and he came to a stream of something running down the mountain, and when he attempted to jump across it. he fell with one foot into it; and that was the way in which he got his foot and leg burned. This Indian came to the fort to get Doctor Barclay to administer some remedy to cure his foot.

From a point on the mountain immediately back of Linnton you can see five peaks of the Cascade range. As we passed from the Atilla [Umatilla?] to Doctor Whitmarsh's [Whitman's ?] we could distinctly see Mount Hood, at the distance of about, one hundred and fifty miles.

CLIMATE.—The climate of this, the lower section of Oregon, is indeed most mild. The winter may be said to commence in about the middle of December, and end in February, about the 10th. I saw strawberries in bloom about the first of December last in the Fallatry [Tualatin?] Plains, and as early as the twentieth of February the flowers were blooming on the hill sides. The grass has now been growing since about the tenth of February, and towards the end of that month the trees were budding, and the shrubbery in bloom. About the twenty-sixth of November we had a spell of cold weather and a slight snow, which was gone in a day or two. In the month of December we had a very little snow, and it melted as it fell. In January we had a great deal of snow, which all melted as it fell, except once, which melted in three days. The ground has not been frozen more than one inch deep the whole winter, and plowing has been done throughout the winter and tall. The ink with which I now write has stood in a glass inkstand, on a shelf, far from the fire, in a house with only boards nailed on the cracks, during the whole month of January, and has not been frozen, as you may see from its good color. As regards rains in the winter, I have found them much less troublesome than I anticipated. I bad supposed that no work could be done here during the rainy season; but a great deal more outdoor work can be done in the winter season than in the Western States. The rains fall in very gentle showers, and are generally what you term drizzling rains, so light that a man can work all day without getting wet through a blanket coat. The rains are not the cold, chilly rains that you have in the fall and spring seasons in the East, but are warm as well as gentle. Since I have been here I have witnessed less wind than in any country I have ever been in; and I have heard no thunder, and only seen one tree that had been struck by lightning. If the tall timber we have here were in the States, it would be riven and blown down, until there would not be many trees left. The rains are never hard enough here to wash the roads or the fields. You can find no gullies washed in the roads or fields in this region.

COMMERCIAL ADVANTAGES.—I consider the commercial advantages of this country as very great. The trade with the Sandwich Islands is daily increasing. We are here surrounded with a half civilized race of men, and our manufacturing power will afford us a means of creating a home market besides. South America, the Sandwich Islands, and California, must depend upon us for their lumber. Already large quantities of shingles and plank are sent to the Islands. We shall always have a fine market for all our surplus; but, until this country is settled, we shall have a demand at home. Most of the vessels visiting the Pacific touch at the Sandwich Islands, and they will be glad to obtain fresh supplies of provisions there. The Russian settlements must also obtain their supplies here. We have China within our reach, and all the islands of the Pacific There can be no competition with us in the way of provisions, as we have no neighbors in that line. I consider Oregon as superior to California. The climate of that country is too warm for men to have any commercial enterprise. Besides, in California, pork and beef can not be put up; and consequently, the grazer loses half his profits. For a commercial and manufacturing people, the climate of Oregon is warm enough. We can here preserve our pork and beef, and we have much finer timber than they have in California, and better water power, and not the drouths (sic) they have there. I do not wish a warmer climate than this. A very warm climate enervates mankind too much.

Towns.—This is a new item in the geography of this country, and one that I have never seen before; but of late towns have become quite common. As all the towns yet laid out in the country are upon the water, I shall begin at the mouth of the Columbia, and come upwards. First, there is old Astoria revived. Captain Applegate and others are now laying off a town at old Astoria, to be called Astoria. They have not yet sold any lots. Next is Linnton, laid off by Burnett and McCown. This place is on the west bank of the Wallamette River, four miles above its mouth, and is the nearest point on the river to the Fallatry [Tualatin] Plains, and the nearest eligible point to the head of ship navigation for large vessels on the Wallamette. Next in order is Oregon City, laid out by Doctor McLoughlin, at the falls. At this place there are four stores, two sawmills, one gristmill, and there will soon be another built by the Doctor, to contain about three run of stones. There is quite a village here. The last, town I shall mention is

Champoe, on the Wallamette, at the head of navigation. I do not know that any Iota have as yet been sold at that place. Business of all kinds done in the territory is very active, and times are flourishing. Lazy men have become industrious, as there is no drinking or gambling here among the whites; and labor meets with such ready employment and such ample reward. that men have more inducements to labor here than elsewhere. This is, as yet, no country for lawyers, and we have the most peaceable and quiet community in the world. Mechanics find ready employment, as well as ordinary laboring hands. Farming is considered the best business in this country. This may be seen at once from the prices of produce, and its easy production. The business of making and putting up butter, which is here never worth less than twenty cents, is very profitable. Good fresh butter, I am told, is never worth less than fifty cents, and often $1 per pound in the Pacific Islands. There are now in operation, or will be this summer, mills enough to supply the population with flour. There are several mills, both saw and grist, in operation up the Wallamette, above the falls. There is no scarcity of provisions at the prices I have stated; and I find that our emigrants who came out last year, live quite comfortably, and have certainly improved much in their appearance. When an individual here has any idle time he can make shingles. which are worth $4 for fir and $5 per thousand for cedar. Any quantity of them can be sold at those rates. We have the finest spar timber, perhaps, in the world, and vessels often take off a quantity of timber for spars. The sawmills at Wallamette Falls cut large quantities of plank, which they sell at $2 per hundred. Carpenters and other mechanics obtain $3 per day and found, and ordinary hands $1 per day and found. The fir timber of this country makes excellent coal for blacksmiths; and what is singular, neither the fir nor cedar, when burned, make any ashes. It has been supposed that the timbered land of this country will be hard to clear up, but I have come to a very different conclusion, from the fact that the fir timber has very little top, and is easily killed, and burns up readily. It also becomes seasoned very soon. It is the opinion of good farmers that the timbered land will be the best wheat land in this country.

[P. H. B.]

1844 November 2

Tualatin Plains [1]

November 2, 1844.

Dear Sir,—

Your communication of the 20th October, 1844, was duly received, and a press of business has delayed my reply till now. In relation to the subject of inquiry contained in your letter (being the natural resources of Oregon), I can truly say that I entertain a very high opinion of the great and decided advantages bestowed by nature upon this most interesting and beautiful portion of our globe.

Our facilities for commercial enterprise are most decided, as the rapidly increasing, commerce of the great Pacific lies at our very door. The climate of this country is more *equable*, subject to fewer extremes than any, perhaps, in the world. I have been here about one year, and have found it most delightful, and I can truly say that it is the most healthy country I have ever lived in. During the present year, I have scarcely heard of a case of fever in the whole country. The timber of Oregon is indeed most superior, and constitutes a large portion of its wealth; and we have not only the tallest, finest timber in the world, but we have everywhere water power to any desirable extent, suitable for propelling all kinds of machinery.

The soil of this country is most excellent, and can be prepared and cultivated with less labor than that of any other country. Wheat is the great staple of the world, and as a wheat-growing country, this ranks in the very first class. The crop is not only of the *best quality, but is always large, and there is no such occurrence as a failure of the wheat crop.* For potatoes, melons, turnips, and garden vegetables generally, our soil is superior. Indian corn does not succeed well, and in fact we have no use for it, as our cattle live all the year upon the natural pastures of the country. Since I have been here, I have been myself engaged in farming occupations, and I have been astonished at the very small amount of labor required to cultivate a farm. Potatoes are planted,

---

[1] William Henry Grey, *A History of Oregon, 1792-1849* (1870), p 411.

and nothing more is done to them until they are ready for digging, when they are not dug, but generally turned up with the plow. Peas are sown broadcast, like wheat, and are neither staked nor cultivated, and produce in great abundance. Plowing is done here from the month of September until July, and wheat is sown from October to May, and potatoes are planted in March, April, and May. A team of two horses, with a very light, easy plow, can break prairie land, but a team of two yoke of oxen is most generally used. I am informed that timothy, clover, and blue grass all grow well in the soil of Oregon. For pasturage this country is preeminent. Horses, cattle, and sheep require neither feed nor shelter, and keep fat all the year round. Hogs are raised here with partial feeding, and pork is generally fattened upon wheat, and finer pork I never saw anywhere.

I omitted to mention in its appropriate place that our harvesting commences about the 20th of July, and continues throughout the month of August; and during the present year we had no rain from about the 1st of July to the 15th of October, so that we had the finest weather for saving our crops imaginable.

One thing that strikes the beholder of this country with greatest force, is the unsurpassable beauty of its scenery. We have snow-clad mountains, beautiful valleys, pure, rapid streams running over pebbly beds, with numerous cascades and waterfalls, and trees of superior grandeur and beauty.

The government of Oregon has grown up from necessity; and perhaps no new organization has been adopted and sustained with so much unanimity and good order. Every circumstance has tended to strengthen it. I attended the last term of the Circuit Courts in most of the counties, and I found great respect shown to judicial authority everywhere, and did not see *a solitary drunken juryman, or witness, or spectator.* So much industry, good order, and sobriety, I have never observed in any community. Our population seem to be exceedingly enterprising, and is making rapid progress to comfort and wealth. As yet, we have had no murders, no robberies, thefts, or felonies of any kind, except one assault with intent to kill. Our grand juries have exhibited very laudable assiduity in discharging their duties, and criminals here will meet with certain and prompt punishment.

Nature has displayed here her most magnificent powers, and our country has its full share of natural advantages. Our prospects are most brilliant. If we can keep out intoxication, *and we will do it,* half a century will not roll away before there will exist in Oregon one of the most industrious, virtuous, free, and commercial nations in the world.

I have already protracted this communication beyond its appropriate length, and will now close it by subscribing myself,

Yours, etc,

PETER H. BURNETT.

Dr. E. White

1844 November 4

Palatine [Tualatin] Plains,

Oregon,

NOV. 4, 1844.[1]

...The emigrants are now daily arriving, and will all be here in a few weeks at farthest, and I expect to receive other letters and papers, which I am informed are on the way. I have now an opportunity to write a hasty letter, as one of H. B. Co.'s [Hudson Bay Company's] ships, the Columbia, leaves Vancouver in a few days, for the Sandwich Islands.

Our country is most beautiful, fertile and well watered, with the most equable and pleasant climate. Our population is rapidly increasing; and. the country is making great progress in wealth and refinement. I have never yet before seen a population so industrious, sober and honest as this. I know many, very many young men, who were the veriest (sic) vagabonds in the states, who are here respectable and doing exceedingly well. Our crops the past year (1844) have been most bountiful, and we have not only a full supply of wheat for our consumption, but a large quantity for exportation. Large numbers of cattle are raised here, which are never fed or sheltered. Many men have from three to four hundred head of cattle. Sheep can be had here in any desirable number, as the H. B. Company have a large flock, and many private individuals have them.

Ere this reaches you perhaps you will have learned that we have a regular government in most successful operation in Oregon. When I

---

[1] This letter was published in *Living Age* September 13, 1845. *Living Age* excerpted it from the *Platte Argus* of August 2nd, 1845. The *Platte Argus* published it with the following note. "Letter FROM PETER H BURNET, ESQ. THE following letter was received yesterday by a citizen· this county, from Mr. Burnet, by the way of Oahua, and forwarded by the American consul. The details will be deemed interesting by his old friends and neighbors, and are indeed of importance to all who take an interest in the affairs of Oregon." The microfilm copy was supplied courtesy of Niedersächsische Staats- und Universtätsbibliothek of Georg-August-Universität, Göttingen Germany.

first reached this region, about a year ago, I thought any attempt at organization might be premature. I had not, however, been here long, before I was convinced that a government of some kind was inevitable, It grew out of stern, inevitable necessity. Our commercial and business transactions were considerable. Difficulties were daily occuring between individuals in relation to their "claims;" the estates of deceased persons were daily devoured, and helpless orphans plundered; crimes were committed, and the base and unprincipled, the reckless and turbulent were hourly trampling upon the rights of the honest and peaceable. A civilized population, numerous as we were, could not exist without government. The thing was impossible. We, therefore, organized a government of our own.

We had no money, no means—I was a member of the legislature. I had most of the business to do. We passed a tax-bill, appointed an assessor, and permitted every man not to pay a tax, if he chose so to do, but if he did not pay, being able, we debarred him from suing in this courts as plaintiff. At the same time we passed acts to protect all bono-fide settlers in their claims to the amount of 640 acres. The tax-bill operated like a charm. Nearly all the whole population paid without hesitation. We selected a tall East Tennessean, Joseph L. Meek, for our sheriff. He had been in the mountains with William L. Sublette for eight or ten years, is exceedingly good humored, very popular, and as brave as Julius Caesar. The very first warrant he had delivered to him, was issued for the apprehension of a very quarrelsome and turbulent man, who resisted Meek with a broadaxe, but Meek, presenting a cocked pistol, took the fellow *nolens volens*. The next, and only case of serious resistance to our laws, was on the part of Joel Turnham, of Mo., son of May Turnham, of Clay county. He had assaulted an individual, and a warrant was issued by a justice of the peace. Turnham was himself constable, and John Edmonds was deputized to arrest him. Turnham resisted with a large butcher's knife, but Edmonds had a pistol with six barrels well charged. He shot Turnham four times, the last ball entering above the temple, when he immediately expired. These are all the obstructions to the administration of justice we have had, and in Edmonds' case, he was fully justifiable in killing Turnham, even if he had no warrant, as T. assaulted him first, and pursued him with great violence to the last.

We have now five counties, and two terms of the Circuit Court in each county in every year. We have but one judge, who discharges the duty of probate judge, chancellor, and what not; in fact we have only as yet circuit courts and justices of the peace. Our government was intended only as provisional, to exist until some regular government could be established. We adopted the statute laws of Iowa, where applicable to our condition and not modified by our legislature.

We are now waiting most anxiously for the result of Pakenham's mission[2], and if the two governments have not settled the question between them, the moment that fact is known, there will be one universal movement made. A regular convention will be held and a constitution adopted, (republican no doubt,) and an independent government put in operation at once. Necessity, will compel us to the step. The population of this country are (*sic*) no doubt desirous to live under the government of the United States, but if she will never do anything for us, we must and will do it for ourselves. The people here are worn out by delay, and their condition becomes every day more intolerable. I speak to you with great candor for you know me, and know that I withhold nothing and disguise nothing. We are well satisfied that the United States government, as well as Great Britain, could not object, and would not object, if we form an independent government for ourselves, situated as we are. Treaties must be made with the Indians, and many other things of importance must of necessity be done.

Our population about doubles every year, and our business trebles. We will soon have a printing-press, and a paper of our own; we can then publish our laws.

The practice of the law has commenced, and I have several important suits on hand.

I have a fine "claim," perhaps among the best in Oregon, situated in the centre of one of the most beautiful prairies called the Palatine [Tualatin] Plains. I am in excellent health, contented and happy. Mrs. B's health has improved, and my children are all well, fat and fine.

Your friend Peter H. Burnet.

---

[2] Richard Pakenham the British agent at that time negotiating the Oregon boundary with James Buchannan.

1847 October 27

Oregon Territory[1]

Oct. 27 1847

Dear Sir,[2]

I received your most welcome communication dated April 23 1847 only a few days since, and hasten to make such reply as my limited time and information will permit. You inform me of a fact that we had learned through many channels, and which has given us feelings of deep sorrow—I mean the fact that no territorial government had been arranged for Oregon. You further state, (what indeed we fear,) that there will be nothing done for us at the next session of Congress. I hope in this opinion we may all be mistaken.

You cannot imagine the dreary and desolate state of feeling that pervades our community, in consequence of our country's neglect and injustice. Is it our country's intention to cast us off and abandon us, in our weakness and helplessness? We consider ourselves as the victims, and the only victims of her neglect. Toward all the world, and to all her own citizens she has not only been just; but to her own citizens especially she has ever, until now, been a kind and watchful protector, and guardian. Wherever they had American sail, her laws rapidly followed; and wherever they went, her protection was over them. But we in Oregon, are singularly and strangely unfortunate. Why should our government select a poor far off and defenseless community of freemen, as the objects of her injustice? It is true we have nothing in the world to plead in our behalf, but the justice of our cause. We had always supposed that this consideration would be ample with our country.

We have no delegate in Congress to raise his voice in our cause, and make known our wants. We cast no votes, and are not permitted

---

[1] Source: c970 f85. From a photocopy of the original by permission of The University of Missouri, Western Historical Manuscript Collection—Columbia, MO.

[2] It appears this letter was sent to James M. Hughes of Liberty MO. He was a congressman in 1843-45.

to pay any taxes. We only enjoy the privilege, (and a great one I admit it is,) to call ourselves American citizens; but we have none of the rights that belong to them. We seem to be beneath the notice of our government—almost "beyond the reach of humanity." And why is this so? Are we not men? Are we not civilized men? Are we not American citizens? Have we wronged our country? Have we committed crimes?

Why Sir, we remember the days of our childhood—the country we left. We have not forgotten the story of her not recent glorious revolution, and her birth as a nation. We learned the incidents of her history, and her principles, from our fathers. Our common ancestors achieved their independence, and left the boon to us of Oregon as well as to you. We have only changed our residence—not our principles or attachments to the government of our country. We have acted under the impression that it was the imperative duty of all civilized governments to afford law and protection to the people, whose allegiance they claim. In other words that there is a mutual obligation binding upon the governing power and the governed; and that while our government claims, and we yield her, allegiance and obedience, she is bound by the immutable and eternal principles of justice, that even a government cannot disregard to give us protection.

Of all the conditions in which a race of civilized men can be placed to be entirely without government, is the most unhappy, and though we in Oregon, have had a mere temporary one, organized and kept up with great difficulty, when we did not even know that our conduct would be fairly appreciated by the two great powers who claimed the country—still we have been kept from one long year to another in that state of painful wearisome suspense, of hope deferred and prospects blighted, which still clings and sticks to us as if a part of our woeful destiny.

I am aware that our country has been for some time engaged in an expensive foreign war, and that the demands upon the Treasury have been and are still heavy. But will this fact justify her in withholding her laws and protection from a defenseless and innocent community? I know if the question regarding the organization of a Territorial government for Oregon is to be decided upon dollars and cents, we are gone. We shall get no government, and perhaps not for years to come. Our government, like Goldsmith's muse, found us poor, and will keep us so. I cannot say how far such a motive has influenced leading men East of the Rocky Mountains. I should never have supposed for a moment that even some of our editors could be under the control of a policy so unjust and niggardly, had I not seen an article in the New York Tribune, of such a stamp. I have not the paper before me, but the substance of the article I remember well. Its character was too strange not to be remembered. The Editor stated in substance that Congress had better let the people of Oregon alone, they were governing themselves very well, that a Territorial government would be expensive, and that the demands upon Uncle Sam's strong box were heavy—but it would however be well for Congress to pass an Act to establish a customhouse at the mouth of the Columbia, that the trade might be equalized between the American and foreign merchants. In other words the editor was anxious that we should feel and bear the burden of government, while we were excluded from all its benefits. He was for taxation without representation. Our country was only to notice us through her taxes. We were to have no representation in her legislative halls, were not to be heard in her solemn courts of justice, and our lives, our reputation, and our honor, were to receive no protection form her. Why Sir, this would be the worst form of tyranny ever known or heard of. Even the slave has the protection of his mother. Even the worst despot will sometimes issue his edicts for other purposes besides taxation.

The people of Oregon are anxious to pay taxes for its support of government. All they ask is that taxation and the blessings of government may come together. So long as our country will tax us as she does her other citizens, we will be content and pay most cheerfully. If we are poor and unable to pay much we will pay as much as we can, and we will use all reasonable exertions to enable us to pay more, whenever our circumstances will permit. We are of the opinion that in a few years under the protection of our country we should be enabled to return any expenditures she may incur on our account. But if our country is only to deal out her justice when she can make a speculation by it, we have nothing to say. We must submit.

I will not occupy your time with a detail of our history here in Oregon; nor will I trouble you more than with a brief statement of the circumstances under which we now find ourselves. For some few of the more prominent facts connected with the history of the settlement here I refer you to the Petition of the people of Oregon, to which you will find my name appended, as one of the committee appointed to draw it up. You will also there find some of the facts stated relative to our present unhappy condition. Other circumstances exist some of which have lately transpired, which deserve a full and ample statement.

Our Indian relations are becoming every day more difficult and delicate. For some years the Indians, residing between the Cascade range of the mountains and the sea coast have been insisting upon payment for their lands, particularly by those claiming the Willamette valley. They have been appeased from time to time by assurance that the United States would send agents authorized to treat with them, and that we have in Oregon had no right to treat, as our government never permitted its people to purchase lands of Indians. As our settlements have rapidly extended, their jealousies have been excited, and their means of subsistence diminished. Our people have settled around their Kamas grounds and our swine have devoured that part of their support. We have been at a loss to know what to do. We could not treat with the Indians nor could we control our own people. All we have been enabled to do, was to put off the evil day yet a little further. Sometime during the last summer some fifteen or twenty Indians ordered some two or three white settlers from their claims, the Indians stating that the white men's hogs were eating up their Kamas. The whites armed themselves, and a conflict was likely to ensue. Gov. Abernethy was sent for, and appeased the Indians by promising them that the U. States Indian Agent would be here in four months, which time has elapsed. The Indians were very loathe to believe the Gov. stating that they heard many such promises, that they were growing old , and their numbers diminished rapidly, and they would all be dead before the government paid them anything. They very reluctantly consented to wait four months longer; and although the time has expired, and we have been looking for trouble none has as yet occurred; owing perhaps to the fact that there is an abundance of acorns this year upon which they have been accustomed to live. This occurrence took place in the Tualatin Plains about 30 miles from Willamette Falls. The Indians on the north side of the Columbia River, have become clamorous for compensation for their lands. Our settlements are extending in that direction and the Indians are becoming more and more jealous. We know if our settlers once commence paying for their claims, that no claim can be taken without paying a high price for it. Had we the right and the means we could make treaties respecting large districts of country at once. Situated as we are we can do nothing but lie upon our claims.

But the Indians in the second region, in the vicinity of the Dalles, Walla Walla, and Dr. Whitman's are likely to become most hostile. Circumstances have occurred of late, which show their true character. Some seven or eight of the recent emigrants just arrived, were encamped near the Dalles in the month of September last; and while there a part of their baggage was taken by the Indians. For the purpose of forcing the Indians to return the articles the Whites seized upon a band of Indian horses. The owners of the horses were perhaps entirely innocent of the theft; but whether they were or not they resisted and a conflict ensued, in which M. Shepherd, a young man from St. Louis, was killed, and two of the white men wounded, and one Indian killed, and perhaps some wounded. The Whites fled, being outnumbered. Governor Abernathy immediately repaired to the scene, and pacified the Indians and all was peace again. Some four weeks afterwards, however, the Indians made an attack upon seven wagons drove away the owners and robbed them of most of their loading. Other wagons have been robbed; and from one they took three thousand dollars cash, besides other things. I am not able to give you a precise number of wagons robbed; not having seen anyone who was present, but that some fifteen wagons have been thus treated is very certain.

These depredations have reached a point of very serious importance; and unless government will do something to prevent their reoccurrence, it is not very difficult to anticipate their increase. Unless prevented by prudent management in future, they must lead, in a very short time, to a general war. The Indians seem to be mainly urged on by a love of plunder; and they have now tasted of its rewards. They will not readily desist unless checked at once. There exists now a crisis in our affairs that demands speedy action upon the part of the U. States.

I have reflected much upon our condition, and upon the best means within the power of the government to manage its affairs in Oregon. It does seem to me, that the United States ought at once to determine whether the Territory of Oregon is worth possessing, and whether they will keep it, or abandon it. If they keep it they must govern it, or disgrace themselves in the eyes of the whole world; and if they govern it, they must begin soon, if they wish to do so upon economical principles. Now I will give you my reasons most candidly for thinking so, and if I do so in a plain and homely style, you will excuse me for the sake of the subject spoken of.

In the first place a statesman cannot alter circumstances. He must look to things as they exist, and not as he would have them. All he can do, is to adapt his conduct to circumstances. We must look to the circumstances that now exist in Oregon to see whether it is not only more just, but absolutely more economical for the general government at once to extend its jurisdiction and laws over Oregon. I am certain in my own opinion that if any sensible individual were vested with the ownership of the colony of Oregon and with the duty of governing it, he would at once set about it. There is no time to be lost, unless indeed the government is reckless of consequences.

To understand our situation it is necessary to look at our geographical position. We are here nearly 4000 miles from the seat of government and 2000 miles from the inhabited bodies of the country we have left, with a wide waste of desert land intervening, traversed by warlike and predatory bands of roving Indians, and destitute of any available means of subsistence for any considerable body of men. We will suppose that a single nation of Indians upon the line of travel should become hostile; it would at once cut off all emigration and travel upon the route. The line of communication by land between this country and the United States must be kept open so long as Oregon is retained by the Government. The cheapest way to do this is certainly to keep the Indians upon or near the line in peace by dealing with them fairly, and by checking the rashness of our own peoples and by cultivating a spirit of kindness and good will between the Indians and the Whites; and also by establishing Military Posts at suitable points along the way.

But by far the most difficult task will be to manage the Indians in Oregon. They are here in contact with the Whites subject to be soured by all those irritating circumstances necessarily arising between two races of men so different in manners, education, habits, pursuits and customs, in a word, between a civilized and a barbarian people. That we will ultimately have an Indian war in Oregon, I have no question. I believe there has been no part of North America ever colonized without such a war. But it is our policy and duty to put it off as long as possible. We are situated like the skillful general whose endeavor it is to avoid an immediate conflict because he is now too weak to meet his rival; but his recruits are constantly coming in, while the army of his adversary is constantly dwindling away.

For the purpose of illustration, we will suppose that an Indian war was now raging in Oregon. What would then be the relative position of the two parties? The agricultural portions of this country lie detached from each other and surrounded by chains of mountains; and our means of intercourse are as yet very imperfect. We have had no time to open roads to all the new settlements. Our population for these reasons is very much scattered, living remote from each other. Our people would be compelled to congregate together at different points, and protect themselves by stockade forts. Our means of subsistence in such cases would be scant. We could not bring our bands of stock together, as the pasturage would be inadequate to their support, and we could not protect them dispersed through the country. We would have no old settlements to rely upon for aid and succor—we would have to rely upon our valor alone. Owing to the nature of the country we would necessarily be compelled to act upon the defence. Had we the power to become the attacking party we could strike a decisive blow at once, and speedily terminate the war.

We will now look upon the other side of the picture, and see what position the Indian would occupy. The various tribes surrounding the White settlements are at peace with each other. So far as my limited knowledge of their history extends that have been in this state for years. The Hudson Bay Company have always encouraged peace among them and have succeeded. The various tribes have a common medium of communication in the "jargon" as it is here called; a language I believe originally invented by the servants of John Jacob Astor for the purposes of trade with the nations; and since adopted by the H. B. Company, and the settlers in Oregon for the same purposes. These circumstances and the natural simplicity of the "jargon" consisting of very few words, have spread a knowledge of it among most of the Indians.

Besides these means of pursuing union and peace among the Indians there have been numerous intermarriages among them; and the small remnants of once powerful and numerous tribes, have amalgamated with the larger divisions. In the second region of Oregon extending from the Cascade Range to the Rocky Mountains, there has for many years existed a still stranger bond of union—I mean a common interest and a common danger. The tribes inhabiting this vast plain, have been compelled, especially since the establishment of Fort Hall, to travel a great distance in pursuit of buffalo, as these animals were never seen nearer the Columbia than in the region around Fort Boises. In their hunts they have often had battles with the Blackfeet Indians. In fact there has existed a war with these warlike Indians for many years. The latter Indians are enemies to all the tribes inhabiting the region I have mentioned. For this and other reasons the Flatheads, Nez Perces, Kiuses, Walla Wallas, Spokans, and other tribes are upon the most amicable terms with each other; and a war with one tribe, unless so managed, as to detach or keep away the others, would involve us with all.

But the number of these various tribes are not only formidable but circumstances and the peculiar advantages of their position render them still more so. This country is better adapted to Indian warfare than any other parts perhaps of North America. The Indians in the second region of Oregon, have any number of the best horses in this country, and such is the mildness of the climate that pasturage can be had at all times, and they would be enabled to attack us at all seasons. Their food besides fish and horse flesh, consists of kamas and other roots, which are abundant every where, and can be collected at any period of the year. The mountains in our vicinity, covered with immense forests of fir and cedar would afford secure places of retreat, where they would be inaccessible to us. To pursue them over there across plains to the mountains beyond would be useless unless we were prepared with better horses than they.

For these and other reasons an Indian war in Oregon is to be prevented so long as we can do so upon honorable terms. We should be greatly injured by such an event; and the United States would have to pay a vast sum of money, perhaps to defray the expenses of the war. Should the Indians manage their operations with secrecy and energy they could annihilate a whole caravan of emigrants on their way to Oregon. It is the part of prudence and true courage to avoid difficulties until they are forced upon us; and then to fight our way through. The people of Oregon, as a whole, have endeavoured to avoid giving any just grounds of offence to the Indians in our vicinity, and we have kept peace so far; but as the number of emigrants increases every year, and the consequent temptations thrown in the way of the Indians are also augmenting the danger of a general rupture; become from year to year more imminent. There is also gradually growing up a bad state of feeling on the part of the Indians toward the Whites, and this arises perhaps from the imprudence of particular persons among both parties. But from whatever cause it arises, this state of bad feeling is on the increase; but by prudent management may be checked and stayed.

The Indians in Oregon although becoming gradually suspicious of the Americans, have not the same animosity toward us as do the Indians upon the borders of the New States. Some years ago, as I am informed, upon good authority, there was a Choctaw Indian (if I am not mistaken as to the tribe to which he belonged) in this country who told the Indians in the second region of Oregon, many horrible tales of the American people, in regard to their treatment of Indians, East of the Rocky Mountains. These stories at the time made a deep impression, and their recollection has not yet been entirely effaced.

It would surely be advisable for our government to pursue peaceable relations with our Indians; not only on account of the Whites, but for the sake of the Indians themselves, as well as for the honor of the country. There is no honor to be gained in a mere Indian war. For this purpose; the government should lay hold of every feeling or attachment entertained by the natives toward us. Suppose that the same state of ill blood existed among the Oregon Indians toward us, as found among the tribes upon the borders of the United States we should be at war in less than one year; and unless prudent measures are pursued here the same state of bad feeling will be brought about. At the present, however, the larger part of the Kiuses, Nez Perce, and other Indians in this vicinity are engaged in raising cattle, horses, and sheep, to a considerable extent, and also in agriculture in a small way; and so long as they remain in these peaceful pursuits they will be adverse to war. They are becoming men of property, have an interest in the preservation of peace, and also an interest in the suppression of robbery on the part of their own people, as their own property will be in danger. Now is the opportune moment for the government of the United States to establish permanent and peaceful relations with the Indians. When once they become fully embittered against us it will require twice the force to govern them. It would seem then clear to me that, aside from the injury an Indian war would inflict upon us it would be a matter of prudent economy on the part of Uncle Sam to attend to his property, and his people at once. A piece of land is much more easily cultivated before it is overrun with weeds than it is afterwards.

From what has been said, some may infer that we in Oregon are very much alarmed at the idea of war. It is true, we do not covet such a boon. We are here in the midst of dangers and we have calmly considered it. We do not admire that fool-hardy sort of courage that is too anxious to get into a scrape, and then still more anxious to get out of it. We admit we have no more courage that theirs, perhaps not so much, but if we should be forced into war we will try to do our duty. We made our way to Oregon through some trouble, wading through a few trials; and we think we have not lost our character, or our courage, although our government seems to consider us beneath its notice. But if we have to fight—my friend and my fellow citizens—we should like to have some authority to fight under, and some flag to follow. I really do not know how we could get along in a battle without a flag. We should not dare to fling to the breeze the "Stars and Stripes," much as we love them, for our country would not permit that. What should we do? Oregon has no flag, and we might disgrace ourselves, with no flag fluttering above our heads, to animate us to deeds of glory. Besides we could make no flag; for there is no device that would be appropriate to poor, deserted, and despised Oregon; except indeed "patience our monument smiling at grief." O that we were out of this abominable predicament! That we had a country! Is there no hope for Oregon! Has she no friends east of the Mountains? Have we no fathers, brothers, friends there?

We are an unfortunate and miserable set of people. We are too insignificant to merit any attention. Before the settlement of the mighty Oregon question, when a rupture with Great Britain was feared, we filled the world's eye. But how fallen! We are now far worse off than we were then. Our country did then care for us. We might, in the event of war, have been useful to feed her armies, and to defend her claim to Oregon. We had paid ourselves the happy compliment to think, that we had, by our residence here constituted, in no small degree, to the settlement of the great controversy; but we were mistaken. We deserve no credit, and no law. Had we sieged upon a few of the H. B. Company's merchant men and Forts, and our government had to pay some several millions of dollars for spoiliations (sic), the laws of the United States would have been over Oregon before this. But we would not do that, or commit any other outrage. We aspired to establish a good character; and where is our reward!

You my friend, have been a good friend to Oregon, and our people are grateful. We are grateful to all our friends. But of what avail is our gratitude, or our regard! The friendship of some men is an injury. It is with us. <u>We are too poor, too far off , too weak and penniless,</u> for our friendship to be anything but a <u>dead weight</u>. Better let us suffer on, friendless and alone. Let the voice of justice sleep. We can turn our wayward steps to those regions of peace, where injustice is never done.

Your friend

Peter H. Burnett

P.S. This is at your service. If the suggestions made regarding our Indian relations be any service, you might transmit them to the War Dpt.

1848 November 8

Juba [Yuba] River Goldmines[1]

Nov. 8th 1848

Mr. Editor:

Knowing from information the interest you take in the prosperity of California, I address this hasty communication to you for the purpose of placing before your readers some intelligence that may be in-teresting to them and to the public generally.

I am one of the wagon party just arrived from Oregon; and the success of our new enterprise has been such as to afford us much gratification. You are no doubt aware of the fact, that our wagons were the first ever brought from Oregon to this country, and that such a project, has until now, been considered impractible (*sic*).

I came to Oregon in the fall of 1843, with the first wagons which penetrated the Dalles, and have had the good fortune to be one of the first party that came with wagons from Oregon to California.

When we were preparing to start, we were aware of the uncertain issue of the attempt, and we prepared ourselves to meet and over-come difficulties not impossible. Our train consisted of some 46 wagons and about 150 men. We were well provided with provisions, and means of every kind necessary to enable us to accomplish the trip.

We left Oregon City about the 10th of September and reached the valley of the Sacramento on the 26th October, seven miles from Capt. Peter Lawson's [Lassen's]. We followed Applegate's Southern route from Fort Hall to Oregon until we came past the little Klamet [Klamath] Lake. We then turned to the right, passing on the east side of New Year's Lake, from which we bore south-east 40 miles to the Sacramento, laid down on most maps as the Pitt [Pit] River. At the point where we struck this stream, we came across a wagon trail made by a party of immigrants from the United States and conducted by Capt. Lawson [Lassen] as pilot.

---

[1] Published in *California Star and Californian,* San Francisco Saturday December 2, 1848 Vol. II, No. 26. Ed. paragraph breaks added.

They had passed about twenty-five days before us. We followed the trail until we overtook this party in the California Mountains, some 40 miles from the Sacramento valley. They had passed the summit of the mountains some 35 miles, without having to make the mark of an axe or spade. From the point at which we overtook the party the only obstruction to our passage down the mountain was fallen timber and loose rock on the surface. Some ten of fifteen hands cut out the road in one day as far as the timber extended—say 15 miles—and did it as fast as the wagons could follow. The loose rock was then the only remaining obstruction, most of which we did not stop to remove, but made our way over them without any serious difficulty than breaking down some two wagons out of fifty.

Some day or two before we took the emigrant party about one-half of them had abandoned their wagons, and started with their baggage packed upon their oxen. We found the pass through the mountains one of the finest natural passes in the world. The ascent and descent are very gradual, and with a little labor an excellent road could be made. All the labor we bestowed upon the road could have been performed by about four men in the space of three or four days.

The worst part of the road from Oregon to California is the pass through the Umpqua mountains, called the Kanyan, on Applegate's route. We found the whole route very well supplied with grass and water. We had one drive of 30 miles to make without water—one of 20 and one of 13.

Our party were exceedingly fortunate. We lost very few animals—most, if not all which, strayed off—and met with no material accident on the way, except one young man was accidentally slightly wounded in the hand with a gun, and another was shot through the wrist with an Indian arrow, in a little skirmish at New Year lake.

The route for wagons is now open, and the approaching year will witness the passage of many wagons from Oregon to California. This route must prove of great benefit to parties of emigrants from Oregon and from the United States.

Yours respectfully

Peter H. Burnett

Part 4

Gold Miner, Political Advocate, Business Agent 1849

THE LETTERS OF PETER H. BURNETT

1849 January 8

MONDAY, January 8, 1849.[1]

The meeting again assembled pursuant to adjournment. The Secretaries being absent, on motion, Robert Gordon was requested to act as Secretary. The committee appointed at the last meeting for that purpose made its report, which, after undergoing a few slight amendments, was adopted, as follows:

"Whereas, The Territory of California having by treaty of peace been ceded to the United States; and the recommendation of the President to Congress to extend the laws of the United States over this Territory has not been acted upon by that body, and the citizens of this Territory are thus left without any laws for the protection of their lives and property;

"And whereas, The frequency and impunity with which robberies and murders have of late been committed have deeply impressed us with the necessity of having some regular form of government, with laws and officers to enforce the observance of those laws;

"And whereas, The discovery of large quantities of gold has attracted, and in all probability will continue to attract, an immense immigration from all parts of the world, as well as from the United States, thus adding to the present state of confusion, and presenting temptation to crime;

"Therefore—trusting in the sanction of the government and people of the United States for the course to which by the force of circumstances we are now impelled, for our own and for the safety of those now coming to our shores:

---

[1] At a public meeting on the 6th January 1849 in Sacramento to consider organizing a Provisional Government Burnett was chosen President. The following is their report on January 8th 1849. It was published in the *Alta California* on January 25th, 1849. The text here is taken from Burnett, *Recollections and Opinions of an Old Pioneer.*

"Resolved, That in the opinion of this meeting it is not only proper, but the present precarious state of affairs renders it very necessary, that the inhabitants of California should form a Provisional Government to enact laws and appoint officers for the administration of the same, until such time as Congress see fit to extend the laws of the United States over this Territory.

"Resolved, That while, as citizens of California, we deeply lament the, to us, unaccountable inactivity toward us by the Federal Congress, as manifested in their neglect of this Territory, yet, as citizens of that great and glorious Republic, we shall in confidence wait for, and when received shall joyfully hail, the welcome intelligence that a proper territorial government has been formed by the Congress of the United States for the Territory of California.

"Resolved, That we fully concur in opinion with the meetings held at San Jose and San Francisco in favor of establishing a Provisional Government, and that we recommend to the inhabitants of California to hold meetings and elect delegates to represent them in the convention to be assembled at San Jose on Monday. 5th March, 1849, at 10 A.M., for the purpose of drafting and preparing a form of government to be submitted to the people for their sanction.

"Resolved, That an election be held by the people of this district, in this room, at 10 A.M. on Monday next, by ballot, for five delegates to represent this district in the proposed convention.

"Resolved, That the President appoint a Corresponding Committee of three persons to communicate with the other districts, and otherwise further the object of this meeting.

"Resolved, That Messrs. Frank Bates, Barton Lee, and Albert Priest be a committee of three to act as judges of the election of delegates."

The report was unanimously adopted.

On motion of Samuel Brannan, a resolution was offered that our delegates be instructed to oppose slavery in every shape and form in the Territory of California. Adopted.

On motion of Mr. Brannan, it was resolved that, in case of the resignation or death of either of the delegates, the remainder be empowered to elect one to fill the vacancy.

The President, in pursuance of the fifth resolution, appointed Messrs. Frank Bates, P. B. Reading, and John S. Fowler, a Corresponding Committee.

On motion of Samuel Brannan, it was resolved that the proceedings of this meeting be published in the "Alta California."

On motion, the meeting adjourned.

PETER H. BURNETT, Pres't.

ROBERT GORDON, Sec'

1849 April 20

The Rights of the People.[1]

To the *Alta California*

MR. EDITOR:

Have the people of California any rights? If so, what is their extent? Have they not certain rights, founded, based, and implanted in man's very nature—that belong to them as men, as human beings—rights that derive no force from human legislation, but trace their origin up through nature to nature's God? Are not these great principles of liberty and justice, that produced the American Revolutionary war, promulgated in the immortal Declaration of Independence, and are now embodied in the American Constitutions, State and Federal, the birthright of every American citizen? I must answer emphatically, they are yet ours, as much so as they were the rights of our ancestors. We have inherited them by direct, clear, and unquestionable lineal descent.

The Federal Government is a government of limited powers—limited by a written Constitution, published to the world, and placed among the enduring and solemn records of the country. The Constitution of the United States not only limits the powers of the Federal Government, but these powers are distributed among three separate and independent departments, the legislative, executive, and judicial. To these departments are assigned different functions, and they were intended by the framers of the instrument to operate as checks upon each other. No one department has any right to assume the powers or discharge the duties assigned to the others. The President is armed with the veto power, to protect his department from the encroachments of the Legislature, and the judiciary has the right to declare the acts of Congress and of the President unconstitutional, null, and void from the beginning. The President is a mere executive officer. He possesses no legislative or judicial power. He can make no law, and construe no law except so far as his mere executive action is concerned.

---

[1] This is a letter written by Burnett about the 20th April 1849 and published in the April 26, 1849 issue of the *Alta California* while Zachery Taylor was still President. Text taken from *Recollections and Opinions of an Old Pioneer*.

The question whether the people of California under existing circumstances have the right to exercise that power inherent in human nature—the power to institute government for the protection of life, liberty, and the right of property—is a question that does not rightfully belong to the executive department of the government to determine; much less does it come within the province of a subordinate military commander. Neither does it belong to any military officer, in time of peace, to decide what code of civil law is in force in this or any other community; nor does he have the right to determine what judicial office is or is not in existence, nor whether this or that individual is rightfully a judicial officer. These are powers foreign to the military office, and not conferred by the Constitution and laws of our country.

Has the President of the United States distinctly and clearly advanced the astounding proposition that, so long as Congress may choose to abandon and, for the time being, abdicate the right of government here, and refuse to extend over us the laws of our country—that so long the most unfortunate and miserable people of California (not having forfeited their rights by crimes against God and their country) have not the liberty to organize a mere temporary government for their protection? Does the President, or any other American statesman, mean to say that, while the people of Oregon had the right to and did organize a provisional government, recognized by Congress itself, the people of California have no such right? I do not understand the President or the Secretary of State as intending to advance any such idea. I know Colonel Benton distinctly advised the people of California to organize such government. The President has not, as I understand, decided that we have no right to institute a temporary government, and that we must submit to the mere de facto government under the military authority; and, had he so decided, he would have done so in derogation of the Constitution and laws of our country. The idea that he has so decided is simply an inference from language that will not, I apprehend, warrant such a conclusion.

What are, in fact, the opinions of the President in reference to the existing state of things in California? In his late message he says: "Upon the exchange of the ratifications of the treaty of peace with Mexico, on the thirteenth day of May last, the temporary governments which had been established over New Mexico and California by our military and naval commanders, by virtue of the rights of war, ceased to derive any obligatory force from that source of authority." I have italicized a part of the above extract for the purpose of more distinctly showing that, in the President's opinion, whatever government existed after the establishment of peace did not so exist "in virtue of the rights of war," and derived no obligatory force from that source of authority.

The President, after speaking of the adjournment of Congress without making any provision for the government of the inhabitants of New Mexico and California, goes on to say: "Since that time, the limited power possessed by the Executive has been exercised to preserve and protect them from the inevitable consequences of a state of anarchy. The only government that remained was that established by the military authority during the war. Regarding this to be a de facto government, and that, by the presumed consent of the inhabitants, it might be continued temporarily, they were advised to conform and submit to it for a short intervening period, before Congress would again assemble, and could legislate on the subject."

All governments, rightfully instituted, must derive their powers from some source. These powers are derivative, not original. The Declaration of Independence assumes the clear and distinct principle that "governments instituted among men derive their just powers from the consent of the governed." Now, according to the above extract, from what "source of authority" did the temporary governments continued after the war derive their powers? Not from the "rights of war." They had ceased. Nor yet from the legislation of Congress, for that body adjourned without any action upon the subject. What then was the source of power? The President says the "consent of the inhabitants." Nor can the President or any one else "presume" this "consent" to be given contrary to the fact and the truth, and does the President mean to say so? Surely not. If the President has the right to "presume" this consent to be given, in direct and positive contradiction to the express acts and declarations of the inhabitants, has he not the right to continue such military government without the "consent" of the inhabitants at all, either actual or presumed?

What is the difference between no consent and "presumed consent" contrary to the truth? Can the President, or any man living, presume away the liberties of the people? Never. If we have no power to dissent, we have no power to consent. We are not free, but mere passive instruments. Suppose a despot should say to a certain people, "I will not exercise despotic power over you without your consent, but I will presume such consent against your express declarations to the contrary." Is it possible that the President of the United States intended to say, in substance, to his fellow citizens of California, "Gentlemen, I will not continue the temporary government established during the war without your consent, but I will presume your consent against your express acts and declarations to the contrary, and, if you attempt to organize a mere temporary government to 'protect you from the inevitable consequences of a state of anarchy, I will put you down by military power, and treat you as traitors and enemies of your country"?

That our military commanders had a right to establish a temporary government "in virtue of the rights of war," to continue during the existence of the war, might readily be admitted; and that the President had the right to continue such government after peace was established, by the "consent of the inhabitants," might be true; and that such consent might fairly be presumed, so long as they submitted to such government, and organized no other, might also be admitted, though doubtful. But to say that the President, a mere executive officer, could continue such government without any actual consent of the inhabitants, and could presume such consent in a manner so violent as utterly to destroy all power of dissent in the neglected people of California, and all power to "protect themselves from the inevitable consequences of anarchy," is to assert a proposition giving to the President a power over his fellow citizens equal to that of a despot.

The opinion of President Polk and that of his distinguished Secretary of State are entitled to the utmost respect, not only upon account of the high and responsible stations they filled, but more especially for the reason that they are both profound jurists and statesmen. But I do not understand them as laying down these two distinct positions—1. That the government continued in California after the war could only exist by the "consent" of the inhabitants; and 2. That the President has the right to presume such consent to be given although it be expressly withheld. Now, both these positions must be sustained before the right can be denied to the people of California to organize a mere temporary government "to protect them," in the beautiful language of the President, "from the inevitable consequences of a state of anarchy."

Mr. Starkie, in his learned treatise on the "Law of Evidence," gives this definition of a presumption: "A presumption may be defined to be an inference as to the existence of one fact from the existence of some other fact, founded upon a previous experience of their connection." After some other remarks not necessary to illustrate the position I am seeking to establish, the author says: "It also follows from the above definition that the inference may be either certain or not certain, but merely probable, and therefore capable of being rebutted by proof to the contrary." (Part IV., p. 1235.)

Now, whether the inhabitants gave, and still continue to give, their consent to the continuance of the military government after the cessation of war, is simply a question of fact. So long as the people of the country submitted to such government, organized no other, and made no objection, by their acts they made that government their own, and their consent might be presumed. But I take it that such presumption is not of that kind called by Mr. Starkie "certain," but only "probable," and "therefore capable of being rebutted by proof to the contrary."

All that I understand the President as intending to advance is, that he had the limited power to continue the de facto government by the consent of the inhabitants; and that so long as they submitted, and did not object to such continuance, nor organize any different government, such consent might be presumed; and for this reason he "advised" the inhabitants to "conform and submit to it for a short intervening period, before Congress would again assemble, and could legislate on the subject." He "advised" (not ordered) the inhabitants to submit. The law commands, and does not advise. And, had the President believed that he had the lawful authority to continue the de facto government against our consent, it would have been his duty to speak "as one having authority," and not merely to give advice.

I have thus, Mr. Editor, spoken my candid sentiments in language, I hope, intelligible and plain. I have done so without intending the slightest disrespect to those of my fellow citizens who may differ with me in opinion. I have only sought to discuss most vital principles, and not to make the slightest personal reflection upon any one. I may or may not trouble you again.

P.

1849 June 18

To the Public[1]

The undersigned, composing a committee appointed at a mass meeting of people of the district of San Francisco, held on the 12th day of June, 1849, to correspond with other districts, and to fix an early date for the election of delegates and the assembling of the convention, and also to determine the number of delegates which should be elected from each district, have given the subject that attention which their limited time and means would permit. The time being a matter, not of principle, but mere expediency, the committee, being duly impressed with the urgent necessity of success in the main object desired by all parties, have not deemed it their duty or right, under the circumstances, to do any act that might endanger the ultimate success of the great project of holding the convention. The committee, not recognizing the least power, as a matter of right, in Brevet Brigadier General Riley, to "appoint" a time and place for the election of delegates and the assembling of the convention; yet, as these matters are subordinate, and as to people of San José have, in public meeting, expressed their satisfaction with the times mentioned by General Riley, and as we are informed the people below will accede to the same, and as it is of first importance that their be unanimity of action among the people of California in reference to the great object to attempt to form a government for ourselves we recommend to our fellow citizens of California the propriety, under existing circumstances, of acceding to the time and place mentioned by General Riley in his proclamation, and acceded to by the people of some other districts. The committee would recommend their fellow citizens of the district of San Francisco to elect five delegates to the convention. And they can not but express the opinion that their fellow citizens of the two great mining districts of Sacramento and San Joaquin have not had anything like justice done them, by the apportionment of General Riley; that they are justly entitled a greater proportion of delegates to the convention than the number

---

[1] This address was a report of a committee drawn up by Peter Burnett. It was published in the Alta California on July 19, 26, and Aug 9 1849. Text taken from: *Recollections and Opinions of an Old Pioneer*.

mentioned in General Riley's proclamation; and the committee, believing their fellow citizens of the mining districts to have equal rights, in proportion to numbers, with the people of other districts, would recommend them to elect an increased number of delegates as in their judgment shall think just and right.

Peter H. Burnett

William D. M. Howard

Myron Norton

E. Gould Buffom

Edward Gilbert

June 18 1849

1849 July 5

July 5th 1849 [1]

Mr. Editor:

There can be nothing clearer to my mind, than the fact, that either Gen. Riley has misconstrued the spirit and meaning of the instructions given him from Washington, or the government has been misinformed as to the correct state of things here, or has "paltered in a double sense" in reference to this subject. Suppose we examine a little and see.

The President, in his late message, after saying in substance that the government established here during the war by our military and naval commanders, in virtue of the rights of war, ceased, after the establishment of Peace, to derive any obligatory force from that source of authority, and that the only government remaining after the war was the one established during the war, then goes on to say, that he regarded this as a de facto government, and that it might be "temporarily" continued by the "presumed consent of the inhabitants." Now, as all powers of government are held to be derivative and not original, since the doctrine of reigning by Divine right has been exploded—and as the de facto government ceased to derive any obligatory force from the "rights of war," it is clear beyond dispute that the President in his message places the "source of authority" in the in the "CONSENT of the inhabitants." And as it is entirely absurd to say at one and the same time that this consent must exist, and yet that it can be "presumed" contrary to the truth and the fact, it is equally clear that if the "inhabitants" should not give such consent, or should withdraw it, then the de facto government would also, in the language of the President, "cease to derive any obligatory force from that source of authority," and would be without authority, and as an inevitable consequence, the inhabitants had, in the opinion of the President, the right to change such government, which rested for its authority alone upon their "consent," and to establish in its stead a mere temporary provisional government, containing nothing contrary to the rights of the United

---

[1] Source: *Alta California* Thursday July 12th 1849. For the date of composition see *Recollections and Opinions of an Old Pioneer*.

States, and to exist temporarily until such time as Congress might make a territorial organization, as was the case with Oregon.

From the order published by Gen Riley at Monterey on the 8th of May last; it appears he is instructed to recognize the de facto government; and he is told that he has not the right to change or modify such government, and that it is his duty to regard it as an existing government until it is changed by "competent authority." Now the phrase "competent authority" in and of itself means nothing. We must refer to something else to know what it does mean. The instructions give no definition. Then we must; look to what the President has said in his message, to know what he would mean by "competent authority." What he has there said in reference to this matter leaves it plain, that as the de facto government rests its authority upon the "consent of the inhabitants," this consent they could refuse to give, or withdraw, and they could organize a mere temporary provisional government, and that the "inhabitants" of California do in fact, in the opinion of the President, constitute this "competent authority."

For one I am ready to admit that the de facto government could be legally and rightfully continued with the "consent of the inhabitants," and that so long as the inhabitants made no objection, and organized no other, their consent might fairly be presumed; but to say that while such consent must exist it may yet be "presumed" against the fact, is a monstrosity that I cannot believe. That the de facto government might be continued until changed by competent authority, I most willing admit. But where and with whom rests this "competent authority."

Now so far as I have seen the instructions from Washington, I do not understand them as at all sustaining the views put forth by Gen. Riley's Proclamation, but are clearly repugnant thereto.

But it seems from a late communication in your paper, under the signature of General Riley, that new instructions have been received, which, he says, sustain the views expressed in his Proclamation. He says: "It may not be improper here to remark that the instructions from Washington, received by the steamer "Panama" since the issuing of the Proclamation, fully confirm the views there set forth; and it is distinctly said in these instructions that "the plan of establishing an independent government in California can not be sanctioned, no matter from what source it may come..."

If these instructions do confirm the views of the Proclamation, I must say that the General has been most unfortunate in his quotation. Although this most solemn and threatening extract from the instructions is put in italics to give it greater point, and introduced in such a connection as to be endorsed as true by General Riley, it contains nothing that touches the question, and only puts forth a libel upon the people of California. As a citizen of the United States, attached to the Government of my country by all the ties of duty, kindred, admiration, and love, as a citizen of California, and as a man, I must express my sincere regret and mortification.

What is meant by the phrase "Independent Government"? Did the intelligent officer who drew up these instructions mean to say that a mere temporary Provisional Government, merely regulating our domestic affairs, and that only while Congress neglected and refused to do so themselves—not conflicting with any rights of the general government—not absolving the inhabitants from their allegiance to the United States—not declaring us independent, but expressly admitting our dependence—in short, such a government as was organized by the people of Oregon and sanctioned by the home government—I ask in candor, did the writer mean to call this an "Independent Government," that could not be sanctioned? I can not believe it. The writer knew too well the use of terms. What is an "Independent Government"? Undoubtedly such a government as was proclaimed by the Declaration of Independence, which declared the colonies to be "free and independent States," and the people to be absolved from all allegiance to the British Crown.—Now, Mr. Editor, let me inquire what single individual in California, not to speak of any considerable portion of this community, ever did propose, or dream of proposing, a "plan of establishing an Independent Government in California?" Is it true that such a plan was proposed? If so, who proposed it? For one, I am not informed of such a thing.

That the authorities at Washington should refuse to sanction a plan for the establishment of an "Independent Government" in California is nothing more than their indispensible duty; and in such a position, the people of this country would most patriotically and willingly support their country with their blood and treasure if necessary. But to say that the people of California, ever contemplated or attempted such a thing, is to charge us with an intent to commit the highest crime known to the laws of the United States, without the shadow of a shade of proof upon which to base such a grievous and most horrible accusation. What the people have done, they have done openly with the best intentions. The government formed in February last, by the people of the District of San Francisco, under the most urgent necessity was only temporary and contained an express prohibition upon the Legislative Assembly to pass any law violating the constitution of the United States, and requiring its officers to take an oath to support that sacred instrument. The project for holding a convention last winter was simply to form a Provisional Government. Most of these things are to be found in the columns of your paper. "The head and front of our offending hath this extent," and "no more." The people of Oregon organized a Provisional Government, and this was sanctioned by Congress and the President, and was not called an Independent Government and the people of California never contemplated any thing more.

The idea of establishing an independent government here—thus cutting us off from the Union and from all protection of the mother country—and erecting a mere petty state to be the sport and play of all the great powers of the world, that might think it their interest or whim to insult and plunder us, certainly never was contemplated by our people here. Why, then, are we charged with such an absurd and criminal attempt? Have the authorities at Washington been deceived as to the true state of things here? How have they come to be so mistaken? There is a great mistake somewhere. Either the people of California are not only too ignorant to govern themselves, as Mr. Clayton of Delaware said, but they are so very ignorant as not even to know what they did attempt or intend; or the authorities at Washington are grossly mistaken.

The unfortunate people of this community have been doomed to suffer. In the first place the United States have neglected us entirely so far as passing laws for our government is concerned, and have only noticed us for the purpose of imposing taxes upon us without representation and without government or laws. They have given us no courts, and have mocked us with sham justice by sending us to Oregon or Louisiana to try all cases arising under the revenue laws, thus practically and for ends of justice, placing all the judicial power in the hands of mere revenue officers, whose decisions must be final in practice and effect. We have had to endure all this, but this is not all. We are now accused of having a plan in view of "establishing an Independent Government in California," and we are warned most solemnly against such a measure, as we had been guilty in truth and in fact. It is surely enough to neglect and still oppress us at one and the same time—but then to slander our reputations—to accuse us of being traitors to our country! Ah! Sir, this is the unkindest, most ungenerous "cut of all"!!

This we must bear also. The right of the injured to complain, is alone left to us. We certainly can protest against such injustice, and for one so long as I live, I will raise my voice in defense of my reputation and my rights. Who is to blame we can not tell. All we know with unerring certainty is, that we are the doomed sufferers. The officers here shelter themselves behind that impenetrable shield called "instructions," and the authorities at home are ignorant of our condition. Is our country or our brethren in the States to be blamed for this? Certainly not. They will yet do us justice. The time is coming when California can have her equal station among the States of the Union, and when her servants can be heard, and her voice regarded.

P.

Part 5

Governor of California 1849-1850

1850 June 1

copy 1

San Jose

June 1st, 1850[1]

J. H. Bean Major General of the 4th Division California Militia

Sir,

I enclose [for] you a printed copy of documents received at the seat of Government in my absence, and relating to the late Indian disturbances on the Colorado.

I have directed the Sheriff of Los Angeles to raise forty and the Sheriff of San Diego twenty men, to rendezvous at Los Angeles on the 22nd day of June 1850 (or as soon thereafter as practicable) armed and equipped as the law directs, and to report to you at the place of rendezvous. The company will choose their own officers. Should it be within your knowledge, that a volunteer company has been formed at Los Angeles or San Diego (as may have been done before this) you will direct the Sheriffs of the two Counties above, not to proceed , and will accept the service of the volunteer company. When the force is organized you will instruct the officer in command to proceed promptly to the ferry upon the Colorado, and pursue such energetic measures as may be necessary to punish the Indians, bring them to terms, and protect the emigrants on the their way to California. Should there be any of the military forces of the United States acting against the Indians the officer in command will act in conjunction with and under the orders of the commander of the Federal troops. You will carefully instruct the officer in command of the State Militia that while it his duty to use the most determined and energetic measures, it is equally his duty to conduct his operation with prudence and with as much humanity as may be consistent with the

---

[1] Source: edited from the original on microfilm. F3753:2 Military Department, Adjutant General, Indian War Papers, F3753 California State Archives. George T. Burrill was sheriff of Los Angeles County and Agoston Haraszthy was sheriff of San Diego County.

legitimate ends and objects of the war. When the objects contemplated shall have been accomplished the company will be discharged. The commander of the company in the absence of an officer of the United States, will report to you and be subject to your orders. Much must be left to his and your discretion, which you will have to use according to circumstances. In the absence of Maj. Genl. [J. H.] Bean, Brig. Genl. [Jose Maria] Covarrubias will execute this order.

>Your obt. Serv't
>Peter H Burnett
>Gov. & Commander in Chief

1850 June 4

/copy/2

San José

June 4th, 1850[1]

Maj. Genl. J. H. Bean

Dear Sir,

Since the date of my communication to you of the first inst., I have received some additional information which leads to the conclusion that as many as one hundred men may be needed. You will therefore, if you deem that number requisite, call upon the Sheriffs of San Diego and Los Angeles for forty men in addition to the Sixty already required, observing the same proportion, as near as may be between the two County. As I stated before, much must depend upon your discretion, as new circumstances will no doubt arise, and I hope you will not hesitate to use it in case it should be required.

                         Your obt. servant

                         Peter H. Burnett

                         Gov. & Comd. in Chief

---

[1] Source: edited from the original on microfilm. F3753:3 Military Department, Adjutant General, Indian War Papers, F3753, California State Archives. George T. Burrill was sheriff of Los Angeles County and Agoston Haraszthy was sheriff of San Diego County.

1850 August 15

San Jose,

Aug. 15, 1850. [1]

To Brig. Gen. A. M. Winn,

Second Brigade, First Division, California Militia:

Sir:

It having been made to appear to me that there is a riotous and unlawful assembly, with intent to commit a felony at Sacramento City, in Sacramento County, you will forthwith order out the whole of your command, to appear at Sacramento City on the 16th day of August, 1850, or as soon thereafter as practicable; and you will take command of the same, and give all the aid in your power to the civil authorities, in suppressing violence and enforcing the laws. Should the force ordered out not be sufficient, you will forthwith inform me accordingly.

        Your obedient servant,

        Peter H. Burnett,

        Governor of California and Com'r-in-Chief.

---

[1] Winfield J. Davis, *An Illustrated History of Sacramento County, California* (1890), http://www.archive.org/stream/illustratedhisto00davi/illustratedhisto00davi_djvu.txt. 2010/10/18.

1850 September 4

/copy /3

San José

Sept 4, 1850[1]

Sir,

I have not received from you any official information in reference to the expedition against the Indians upon the Colorado. From the difficulty of communication, I presume your reports must have miscarried.

I had learned from unofficial sources that the Indians were not so hostile as expected, and that troops of the United States would be sent to the spot. I had also learned from like sources that the expedition had failed from the impossibility of procuring the requisite number of men; and subsequently did not deem any order from me to disband the troops necessary or proper. From a communication written by Genl. Morehead dated August 8th 1850, and addressed to the Hon. Richard Roman I am left to suppose that some troops of the State are still kept in service. Should this be so, you will issue orders to have them disbanded without delay.

I shall send different copies of this communication by different conveyances that at least one of them may reach you.

                    I have the honor to be

                    Your obt. servant

                    Peter H Burnett

                    Gov. & Comd. in Chief

To Maj. Genl. J. H. Bean

4th Div. Cal. Mil

---

[1] Source: edited from the original on microfilm. F3753:7 Military Department, Adjutant General, Indian War Papers, F3753, California State Archives.

1850 October 25

Sacramento City

Oct 25th 1850[1]

William Rogers Sheriff of the County of El Dorado in the State of California:

You will call out the identified able bodied militia of your County armed and equipped and permit them when collected to choose their own commander... You will cause them to assemble at as early a day as practicable and the officer in command will proceed to punish the Indians engaged in the late attacks in the vicinity of Ringold and along the emigrant trail leading from Salt Lake to California. He will offer any assistance in his power to protect the emigrant and all others traveling the route. He will not keep more men in command than may be indispensable to accomplish the object intended, and disband them at the earliest day when the same shall have been accomplished.

He will use all necessary caution and energy and will report to me through Brig. Gen. Winn of Sacramento City. You will cause a copy of this order to be received in his hands should a different person from yourself be elected to the command.

Your obt. servant

Signed Peter H Burnett

Gov. & Com in Chief

---

[1] Source: edited from the original on microfilm. F3753:9 Military Department, Adjutant General, Indian War Papers, F3753,California State Archives.

1850 November 13

San Jose

Nov 13th 1850[1]

Sir,

Enclosed I send you communications for Commander Rogers which you will please forward.[2]

     Your obt. ser't

     Peter H Burnett

     Gov. & Com in Chief

To

Brig. Gen. A. M. Winn

Sacramento City

---

[1] Source: edited from the original on microfilm. F3753:25 Military Department, Adjutant General, Indian War Papers, F3753, California State Archives.

[2] The Adjutant General notes this letter was sent by express and that the orders to Rogers were missing.

GOVERNOR OF CALIFORNIA

1850 November 15

San Jose

Nov 15th 1850[1]

To Wm. Rogers

Commander of the expedition in El Dorado County.

Dear Sir,

From recent information I am well satisfied that one hundred men are sufficient to protect the people of El Dorado County from further Indian depredations. You will therefore at once reduce your command to that number. You will be careful to make a further reduction whenever circumstanced will justify. You will see from the Original Order under date 25th Oct. that only 200 men were to be raised and no more of them kept in the field than might be necessary. Much must be left to your direction as you have superior sources of information. But every effort should be made to terminate the difficulty as early as possible and with as little expense to the State as practicable.

                        I have Honor to be

                        Signed Your obt. servant

                        Peter H Burnett

                        Gov. & Com in Chief

---

[1] Source: edited from the original on microfilm. F3753:27 Military Department, Adjutant General, Indian War Papers, F3753, California State Archives.

1850 November 15

San Jose

Nov. 15th 1850[1]

Brig. Gen. A. M. Winn.[2]

Dear Sir,

I am this moment in receipt of your communication of the 11th inst. In reply I have enclosed you orders for Commander Rogers which you will promptly forward. That there may be no miscarriage I send one copy by express and one by mail.

                    Your obt. servant

                    Peter H Burnett

---

[1] Source: edited from the original on microfilm. [F3753:26] Military Department, Adjutant, Indian War Papers, F3753. California State Archives.

[2] Albert Maver Winn, President of the Sacramento City Council. Commissioned as Brigadier General in the California Militia by Governor Burnett in April 1850.

Part 6
Lawyer 1850-1857

1852 April 26

Alviso

April 26 1852.[1]

Mr. Buckly (*sic*),

Dear Sir,

I send my sons John and Armstead to school this morning. You can put them at such branches as you may find advisable.

Mrs. B and myself were Protestants until they were about the ages of 11 and 9, and consequently they still retain some prejudices against our religion. All the relations are Protestant and all of their associations. I have pursued a very delicate course towards them, as Christ like to win them gently.

Your own discretion will enable you to understand their feelings.

Yours truly

Peter H. Burnett

---

[1] Source: edited from a photocopy of the original. By courtesy of Santa Clara University Archives, 3DB01, papers of John Nobili, S. J. 1851-1856. Box 1, f16, Burnett.

1852 September 6

San Jose (California)[1]

Sep 6 1852

L. J. Cist Esq.

Dear Sir

I am receipt of your favor of the fourth of July last, and I must cheerfully comply with your request.

I duly appreciate the compliment you pay our "young sister California." To me any just estimate of her merits is peculiarly grateful, and I hope our fellow citizens East of the Mountains will ever entertain a true opinion of the importance of California. In the future historical picture of the world, she is destined to occupy a most prominent place. Neither Jerusalem on the day of Pentecost, nor the city of Rome, in the days of the Caesars ever contained a greater variety of the human race, than does California at the present moment. At this point representations from all the nations of the earth are assembled. What will be result of this new and wonderful state of things no one can certainly foretell. Whether civilization and Christianity will still travel Western until they ultimately make the circuit of the globe, and reach their original seats in the older world, and whether the "end of the world" will then come, and what means and what time will be required to bring these things to pass, the future alone can determine. That great and mighty events in the history of our race are past before us there can be little doubt.

      I have the honor to be

      Your Ob't Ser't

      Peter H Burnett

      1st Gov'r of California 1849

---

[1] From a digitized copy of the original. http://bancroft.berkeley.edu/Exhibits/ Looking/015alg.html. 2009/

1855 August 13

San Jose,

Aug. 13, 1855[1]

Rev. Father Congiato,

My Dear Sir,

I am engaged in study and composition. I wish to give to the world my reason for becoming a Catholic, and I wish to guard carefully against any errors. I wish therefore to consult you, and your learned and pious associates, in regard to a few points at this time and to submit my work to whatever authority our good Archbishop may appoint, when the work is finished. I have investigated the question so closely that the work will be much longer than I at first supposed. I put my inquiries in the form of questions.

1. The tribunal established to decide ecclesiastical causes under the Jewish dispensation was infallible, and its decisions final and conclusive. This I understand to be the opinion of all our divines. Is there a single instance mentioned in the Old or New Testament where this tribunal rendered an erroneous decision except in condemnation of Christ?

2. Is it agreed upon by our divines as to the exact time when this divine protection was withdrawn?

3. Christ reproaches the Scribes and Pharisees with making void the law of God in certain respects by their traditions. Were these traditions or opinions simply the acts of individuals, or were they the legitimate decisions of this tribunal?

4. Was the question regarding the character of Christ's then future Kingdom on earth, (that is, whether temporal or spiritual) a matter of faith with the Jews? And had this tribunal ever decided that question? And, if so, what was the decision?

5. Is there any recorded instance where the divine protection was expressly promised to this tribunal?

---

[1] Edited from a photocopy of the original, by the courtesy of the archives of the Jesuit Province, Saratoga, California.

6. Do the <u>offices</u> established by Christ and his apostles still exist in our Church, and only those offices?

7. What is the difference between a bishop and an archbishop?

8. What is the peculiar character of a Cardinal as distinguished from other clergy?

9. Are not the <u>additional functions</u> conferred upon Archbishops, Cardinals, and Legates, but <u>a part</u> of the powers rightfully belonging to the Pope, and <u>conferred by him</u> to aid him in discharging the duties peculiar to his office?

In the controversy between Bishop Hughes and Mr. Breckinridge, some of these questions were raised and left undecided. If no exact time is fixed upon by our Church as to when the divine protection was withdrawn, then I suppose it is left as matter of opinion.

If you can give my answers to these questions without trespassing upon your other duties, I will thank you very kindly.

My respects to Fathers Nobili, De Vos, and all the others.

                    Yours truly,
                    Peter H. Burnett

Part 7

Author, Supreme Court Judge
1857-1862

1859 May 17

San Jose,
May 17th 1859[1]

Most Rev. John B. Purcell

My dear Sir,

I have completed my work, and by this steamer will forward the manuscript to my publishers, Mess. D. Appleton & Co. New York. I could not get any Catholic House to publish the work, owing to different causes. I presume it will appear toward the close of 1859. I have had it critically examined and appraised, by the Jesuit Fathers of Santa Clara College, especially by Father Cicitari [Felix Ciccateri S.J.], the President who is a very profound theologian, scholar, and critic. I hope and pray it may do some good. Time will show. I think I can truly say it is Catholic in sentiment and spirit. I have studiously endeavored to be plain, clear, and certain. I suppose Mr. Campbell and some others, whose positions I have freely examined, may complain. But if they should, I think they will do so without sufficient reason. I have spoken boldly but courteously. I am not ashamed of the Faith, and I am ready manfully to avow it. I will direct my bookseller to send you a copy.

I have dedicated the work to you, upon condition that you consent. I have instructed my publishers, that in case you should object, they must omit the dedication. But I hope you will not object. I annex the form of the dedication, and assure you that it contains nothing but the truth. There is no flattery in it. It is plain truth—no more. I think it is fitting that it should be dedicated to you. You made me a Catholic, and I claim you as a Father in Christ. I have a right to do this have I not? And I feel grateful for the greatest of all blessings.

My dear Archbishop, when I went to Oregon in 1843, I was in debt about $20,000; and the then great purpose of my life was to pay up every cent, that I might be just to all men. I succeeded in paying

---

[1] Source: edited from a digitized copy of the original of Peter H. Burnett to Archbishop John Baptist Purcell, 17 May 1859, Archdiocese of Cincinnati Collection II-4-o, University of Notre Dame Archives.

interest and principal. The next great purpose of my life, was to publish my reasons for becoming a Catholic; and this purpose is now about finished, so far as my own labors are concerned, unless some accident should occur. What great end to aim at next, I can scarcely conceive, unless it is to prepare for death. Having retired from public life, and having leisure, I would wish to do all the good I could in any just way. But I am at a loss to know what to strike at next. When I had paid off all my old debts I felt almost lost, for a time. I suppose it will be so now that I have finished my work. But I trust in God. I know it will all be right. For some years I have had the implicit belief that all things would turn out the best for me, and, so far, I have not been disappointed. I have trusted in our Lord with faith and love, and have had every reason to be grateful.

I hope you will live long to discharge your onerous duties to your flock, and that you may be able to bring many wanderers home to the Old Church. Pray for me.

>   Your son in
>
>   The true Faith
>
>   Peter H. Burnett

To The

Most Rev. John B. Purcell
Archbishop of Cincinnati,

Whose arguments laid
The foundation of
My conversion to
The Old Church

This work is dedicated
As evidence of
the gratitude of
His son in
The True Faith

The title of the work is:

The
Path
Which led
A
Protestant Lawyer
To The
Catholic Church,

By
Peter H Burnett

"Thou hast made us, O Lord, for Thyself and our hearts are restless, until they repose in Thee."

Saint Augustine.

1859 December 1

New York,

Dec. 1, 1859[1]

Most Rev John B. Purcell,

Dear Sir,

I arrived in this city on yesterday for the purpose of superintending the publication of my work. It will soon be out, and has already been announced as in press. I will thank you if you will suggest to me the name of a faithful agent in your city and the number of copies I had better send at the beginning. The work is stereotyped, and I can have any number published I wish. I will send to each Bishop and Archbishop in the U.S. a copy, and I may be able ultimately to send a copy to many of our literary and religious institutions. I hope it may do some good.

Yours truly

Peter H. Burnett

P.S. Direct to care of Appleton and Co.

---

[1] Source: edited from a digitized copy of the original of Peter H. Burnett to Archbishop John Baptist Purcell, 1 December 1859, Archdiocese of Cincinnati Collection II-4-o, University of Notre Dame Archives.

1859 December 25

New York

Dec. 25 1859[1]

My Dear Archbishop,

I rec'd your note of the 19th inst and your requests shall be all attended to promptly. They are now printing the first 1,000 copies 300 of which I will send to California and Oregon. It will take the remainder of Dec. to finish the printing, and the binding will take some ten days. So the work will not be out before the 10th Jan. It is necessary for me to be here while the printing is going on. I regret I could not be with you on this day. But my heart is with you. I will not fail to visit you sooner on later, if my health will permit.

I was at the Fair held in this City for the aid of the Sisters of Mercy, and I attended 6 nights in succession, and on the 7th I attended the lecture of Dr. Cahill and caught a severe cold, from which I have not recovered.[2] I have been so long in the genial clime of Cal. that I find my nose and cheeks frost bitten already, even from the little exposure I have encountered in walking the streets of this bustling city.

I feel much gratified at the interest you take in my work. I trust it may be found worthy. I have taken every precaution I could to make it strictly Catholic. I think I may say there is no faltering support given the Old and beautiful Church. The work is elaborate and contains either a great deal or nothing. It is no halfway production, to the best of my poor judgment. It has only been read by two persons outside the Church, and has led to the conversion of one, and the other, the proof reader in this city, asked me for a copy when published, saying he liked it much and was inclined to my view of the question. God grant that it may do good, and that his poor servant

---

[1] Source: edited from a digitized copy of the original of Peter H. Burnett to Archbishop John Baptist Purcell, 25 December 1859, Archdiocese of Cincinnati Collection II-4-o, University of Notre Dame Archives.

[2] Daniel William Cahill, Irish lecturer and controversialist. In December 1859 he visited the United States and lectured on Astronomy and other scientific subjects.—*Catholic Encyclopedia*. Ed.

may not have lived in vain. I felt all and more than I expressed, "My heart is in the coffin there with Caesar."

Give my very best respects to Mr. and Mrs. Springer, and accept for yourself the love and submission of

Your Son in the True Faith

Peter H. Burnett

1860 January 3

New York,

January 3, 1860.[1]

Dr. O. A. Brownson,

My dear Sir,

I intended to have visited you at your home, but as my health has been so poor that I could not do so, and now I am compelled to leave this climate and return to Cal. by the Steamer of the 5th Inst. My health has been steadily declining for some weeks, and for the last ten or twelve days, I have had a bellglass face that is wearing away my constitution inch by inch. I may return in the Spring. I am just able to write, but with labor. I have directed, Mess Appleton and co to send you a copy of my work, which I hope you may find time to review. You will find that my quotations are from the English Protestant Version. My reasons were these

1. Fidelity to my undertaking to give the path which led me to the Church as stated in the Preface

2. The work is mainly intended for the Protestant reader

3. In reference to the main points of my argument I found the version of King James more strongly in my favor. For example, the two quotations from the last chapter of Hebrews, and the one where St. Paul tells Titus to reject a heretic. The word reject is much more decisive of the governing power of Titus than the word avoid. There are other examples, but these are all that occur to me now and I cannot examine.

I had the work carefully examined and appraised by two different Presidents of Santa Clara College, the leading Institution in our State, and which is under the direction of the Jesuit Fathers. It is published now in the form in which it was finally approved, with the exception

---

[1] Source: edited from a digitized copy of the original of Peter H. Burnett to Orestes A. Brownson, 3 January 1860, Orestes Augustus Brownson Papers I-3-o, University of Notre Dame Archives.

of two short notes. I have done all I could to prevent errors against the Faith appearing in the work.

I make these explanations in order to be understood. If the work should possess any merit, its circulation should not be retarded for want of our explanation. You have been the victim of misrepresentation, and I anticipate the like result for myself.

Give my best respects to Miss Sarah. I was attending the Fair nightly, and among the multitude I knew no one, when I was accidentally informed that your daughter was there.

Mr. Ryland, my son-in-law who called with me to see you in 1856, and who since became a devoted Catholic, desires me to give you his best respects. Only two persons outside the Church have read my work. The first, Mr. Ryland to whom I read only the main chapters and he became a convert to the Faith. The second, Mr. DeGenat the proof reader in the printing office of John St. Jean 379 Broadway and he applied to me for a copy saying he liked my manner of expressing my views, and was inclined to concur in them. These incidents give me some hope that the work may do at least some good.

Remember me in your prayers.

Yours truly

Peter H. Burnett

Dr. O. A. Brownson

January 4. I had requested my friend Mess A. and co to procure me a passage but they declined doing so upon the ground that I'm not in a condition to go to sea. So I have determined to remain longer. I feel better today.

P.H.B.

1860 January 25

New York,

January 25/60[1]

Most Rev. John B. Purcell

Dear Sir,

While they were striking off 1,000, copies of my work, I obtained one copy for myself; but knowing that it would be some time before the work could be bound, I determined to send you the unbound copy, which I presume you have received. I likewise gave direction to Miss Axco to send you a bound copy for me, which you will no doubt receive in a few days. I also gave them directions as to the copy for Dr Huntington,[2] and the 50 copies for yourself. The work is now out, though it has not yet been advertised. It is well executed.

I have been unwell most of the time since I arrived, and I find it necessary to return to Cal. by the steamer of the 5th Feby. as I cannot, I fear, stand the month of March in this climate. I am still feeble, but able to go about. I cannot say that I can accomplish any further good by remaining here longer. I should like to see you very much, but I fear to take the trip to Cinn. [Cincinnati] in my present condition.

As I shall be in Cal. where I shall not have any opportunity to know what attacks may be made upon my work; and as I may hereafter wish to publish a second edition of or a sequel to it, I must ask of you the favor to send me such criticisms as you may think worthy of any consideration. I have sent a copy to Alex. Campbell, and I wish to send one to Dr. Rice, who had the debate with him at Lexington, but I cannot find out where Dr. Rice resides. I expect attacks from the Protestant press, and some from our own. I am prepared, I trust, to submit with patience to any and everything that may come. If the

---

[1] Source: edited from a digitized copy of the original of Peter H. Burnett to Archbishop John Baptist Purcell, 25 January 1860, Archdiocese of Cincinnati Collection II-5-a, University of Notre Dame Archives.

[2] Probably William Reed Huntington an Episcopal priest and author.

work is wrong, it might to (*sic*) be condemned, if right, it cannot be confuted.

When you shall have made up your mind as to the character of the work, I will thank you to state frankly your opinion. If I am incompetent to render any service to the great Old Church as an author, I wish to know it, that I may walk in my proper sphere.

I saw the Rev. Dr. Cahill to-day for the second time. He is not well, and has determined not to preach any more, as his constitution will not stand it. He is a noble soul; and is overburthened (*sic*) with company.

Give my respects to Sister Loyola, at the convent of the Sisters of Notre Dame. I knew her in San Jose, Cal. and she will remember me.

My dear Archbishop I ask your benediction and your prayers, that I may be humble and patient under all circumstances.

Your Son in the True Faith

Peter H. Burnett

1860 February 2

Bixby's Hotel,
N.Y. 834 Broadway[1]
Feb. 2, 1860

Most Rev. John B. Purcell

My Dear Sir,

I have just rec'd and read yours of the 30th. ult. and am truly grateful that my poor efforts have met with your approbation. The highest and holiest principle in heaven and earth is inflexible loyalty to the truth. And loyalty to truth, with me, is loyalty to the glorious Old Church.

As yet, there have appeared no criticisms in the Press of this City upon the work. The copies were not distributed here as early as the one you rec'd. Mr. Mullaly informed me yesterday that he had written a review of the work, but it was crossed out of the *Metropolitan Record* for the present month, but will appear in the next number.

I sent Arch. Hughes a copy, and rec'd from him a letter under date of 26th ult. in which he says:

"I have run over the contents—and many of the pages of your treatise. I am much pleased with it. I think it will do much good to Catholics as well as Protestants, and will prove to be a valuable contribution to our incipient literature, for, I have observed that it is written with a care and precision which is not always in the power of less experienced writers or less acute intellects, to apply.

"I congratulate you and the Catholic public on this production."

I have written His Grace for permission to publish it, if he has no objections, but have not yet rec'd a reply from him, as he is quite unwell.

I have sent out a number of copies, one to Dr. Bellows, and Dr. Forbes[2], one to Dr. Brownson, and to Dr Ives, and to each of the

---

[1] Source: edited from a digitized copy of the original of Peter H. Burnett to Archbishop John Baptist Purcell, 2 February 1860, Archdiocese of Cincinnati Collection II-5-a, University of Notre Dame Archives.

Archbishops Kenrick etc., and will send a copy to the *London Tablet*, London *Weekly Register*, *Dublin Review*, *Catholic Telegraph*, Dublin, *The Atlantis*, Dublin, *Dublin Freeman's Journal*, *L'Univres*, Paris, *L' Ami de la Religione*, Rome[3], and *Giornale de Roma*, Rome. I also sent a copy to Cardinal Wiseman, with an explanatory letter.

That holy convert Dr. Ives called to see me yesterday. He had just rec'd the copy intended for him. He remained with me about two hours. I have been twice to his house. I have not yet rec'd the notice and letter of your brother.[4] I presume they were directed to the care of Miss. Axco and I have not been there today inconsequence of the cold weather.

I do not anticipate a rapid and extensive sale of my work. I did not suppose that I would make anything by its publication, and I am content to learn any less that may happen. My actual money expenditures upon the work, including the expense of this trip, amount to about $2,500. But they are all paid, with the exception of some $1,000, and if I can bring one soul to the true faith I am fully rewarded. So I receive the approbation of My Church I am happy. The idea that a poor layman like myself should be able to do anything for the cause of presented truth, is consoling to me.

I hope my dear Archbishop you will pray for your son in the faith, and should you depart out of this world before me, I pray you to remember the entreaty of Celsus to his spiritual father (which I think you will find quoted page 693 or 679 of my work[5].) and consider the request as made by:

    Your affectionate son in the True Faith

    Peter H. Burnett

---

[2] Although there is no contextual evidence for transcribing the names as Bellows and Forbes we suspect Burnett sent copies to Henry Whitney Bellows editor of the *Christian Inquirer,* and John M. Forbes who converted to Catholicism but later left the priesthood to which he had been ordained by Bishop Hughes of New York. Ed.

[3] L'Ami de la Religión, Paris.

[4] Fr. Edward Purcell

[5] The quotation from Celsus referred to by Burnett is, "When therefore, in the day of thy liberation, thou shalt first present thyself before the face of Christ...by the mercy of the Lord, then bear in mind thy child Celsus.

P.S. Please present my best wishes to Sister Loyola. My children remember her with great affection. Give my respects also to your brother and to Mr. and Mrs. Springer.

Hon. P. H. Burnett 2nd Feb. '60 PHB

1860 March 29

San Jose,

March 29th 1860[1]

Most Rev. John Baptist Purcell

Dear Sir,

I arrived at home safely on the 3rd Inst. You will have seen, I presume, in the *Metropolitan Record* of the 11th July an extract of a private letter from Arch. Hughes to myself. I did not publish any extract from your letter to me, or from that of Arch. Kenrick of Baltimore, because there was no express consent given, (as was by Arch. H.) and I feared I might violate your intentions. If entirely proper, I would be glad to have your consent to publish an extract from your private letter to me.

My dear Archbishop, I have reflected much upon the question of the personal inspiration of each apostle as to judicial questions, and am satisfied that you are right. But whatever my private opinion might be, I would not take any position against your advice. Conceding this position i.e. the personal inspiration of each apostle as to judicial questions, I must ask your attention to another proposed view, which, it occurs to me will make all clear and consistent.

1. The question decided by the Council of Jerusalem was either a legislative or judicial question, as it could have been no other. A legislative question is, what shall the law be, and refers alone to the future, while a judicial question is, what is the law, and refers only to the present.

2. This judicial question as to the materiality of circumcision was decided by St. Paul.

3. An appeal was taken to the Council and the case reheard upon its merits.

Now it is a universal principle with Courts of justice never to review a decision of a court of final resort; because, in the

---

[1] Source: edited from a digitized copy of the original of Peter H. Burnett to Archbishop John Baptist Purcell, 29 March 1860, Archdiocese of Cincinnati Collection II-5-a, University of Notre Dame Archives.

contemplation of the theory of government, the decision of a court of last resort is always correct, and always final as to the particular case, and the court will not do an idle and vain thing. In the nature of things, Courts must be either of inferior or of superior jurisdiction. A court maybe of both original and final jurisdiction as the S.C. [Supreme Court] of the U.S. in cases affecting ambassadors etc. but they must be of inferior or superior jurisdiction or they cannot be courts at all.

That St. Paul did decide a judicial question that an appeal did lie (*sic*) from his decision to that of the Council—and that the case was reheard upon its merits and finally settled by the decree of that tribunal, would seem to be true. The act of the Council was not idle in exercising actual appellate jurisdiction upon a case decided, in the first instance, by St. Paul. Conceding the individual infallibility of St. Paul in reference to the judicial question determined by him, how shall we account for the final action by the Council? Only, as I conceive, in two ways.

1. From a desire to give satisfaction to others.

2. Because, though individually infallible, St. Paul had only original and not final jurisdiction of the case.

The latter explanation seems to me the better one of the two, though both may be correct.

Suppose a Protestant jurist to oppose my argument in support of the Primacy of St. Peter in this way, "You concede the personal inspiration of each apostle in his capacity of witness and teacher; that is , in reference to both questions of fact and law. Now the voice of the Holy Ghost is equally infallible, whether it speaks through a single medium or through many. For what purpose, then, was superior power given to St. Peter? He could not be more infallible than any other infallible apostle. Infallibility cannot be improved."

I would answer in this way. "I distinguish between qualification and jurisdiction. In the beginning of Christianity, under the peculiar circumstances then existing, it was expedient to give personal inspiration to each apostle both as a witness and as a teacher, but the Church once well established, this personal inspiration was not required, and the inspiration was continued to the corporation, and not to each individual successor of the apostles. But as Our Lord established a permanent system, having permanent offices, with permanent powers belonging to them, He gave the individual apostles only original not final jurisdiction; and for that reason the appeal was permitted from the decision of St. Paul to the Council of Jerusalem. While each individual apostle was inspired, it is equally certain that the Council of Jerusalem was inspired as the organ of the entire Church. Inspiration is a qualification, and is distinct from and independent of the question of final jurisdiction which is the jurisdiction of power. Each individual apostle might well be inspired as to judicial question, and yet not possess final jurisdiction of all cases. Under my theory all is clear and consistent; and the act of the Council in rehearing the appeal from St. Paul was not idle. But under your theory of the personal inspiration of all the apostles, and of their perfect equality as independent officers, how will you justify the Council of Jerusalem in entertaining an appeal, not only from the decision of an infallible apostle, but from one having final jurisdiction of the case? The Council of Jerusalem was intended to give us an instance of the proper exercise of the permanent powers and qualification of the final tribunal of last resort in the Church."

I propose this view at this early day, that I may be ready to answer such an objection, and to turn it against the objector, should it be made. But I will not take such a ground until I have obtained the sanction of the prelates of my own church. I have not sufficient boldness to attempt a new ground, not approved by those who are placed over me. I, therefore, desire that you would keep the question in mind, and when opportunity offers, consult other prelates about it. Should the objection be made, I will at once inform you, and ask the result of your examination etc.

My work has been favorably received in Cal. and sells rapidly. I pray it may do some good. I am gratified that it has met with the approbation of the prelates of my own Church. I expect the determined opposition of the sects and do not fear that.

Give my best respects to Mr. and Mrs. Springer and to your brother, from whom I did not receive the letter you mentioned as having been written by him to me.

Pray for your son in the faith.

Yours in Christ.

Peter H. Burnett

1860 June 8

San Jose

June 8 1860[1]

Dr. O. A. Brownson,

Dear Sir,

I enclose you a review of Dr. Huntington's work, which I submit to you for inspection and publication in your discretion.[2] It substantially contains the leading positions of my late work *The Path to the Church*, and in several instances I have extracted the very language of the work because it was my view and I found these ready for my use. I have put my initials to the production that no one may be responsible but myself. I supposed that I might be able to lessen your assess labors, and bring before the reader in a concise but clear and definite form the main features of an argument that seems to be conclusive. Whether I have done so or not, I am incompetent to determine, and must leave you to judge. I beg of you to pardon the liberty I have taken without first consulting with you. When I returned home, I found my private affairs so confused, that I had to give them my whole attention, except one week's time which I have given to the article I send you.

I am now suffering from an attack of neuralgia, and can barely write. As I never intend to practice my profession again, and have time on my hands, I am at a loss to know how to employ it in the service of the Old Church. My heart is with her. My judgment is with her. How shall I serve her best? That's the question.

Give my respects to Miss Sarah and the family.

Yours truly

Peter H. Burnett.

---

[1] Source: edited from a digitized copy of the original of Peter H. Burnett to Orestes A. Brownson, 8 June 1860, Orestes Augustus Brownson Papers I-3-C, University of Notre Dame Archives.

[2] Probably Rev. Frederick Dan Huntington. Ed.

1860 June 22

San Jose,

June 22, 1860[1]

My dear Archbishop,

I rec'd, on yesterday, your letter of 28th May. I remember Bishop Wood very well. His appearance and superior intelligence made a lasting impression on my mind. I did not know, however, that he had been appointed Bishop. I have not seen the article from the *London C. Standard*, or any other from the English Press. I sent a copy of my work to the Holy Father.

From your letter, I am not certain that I expressed myself in terms sufficiently clear to be distinctly understood. As I kept no copy I will restate the points as distinctly as I can.

1. Christ having exercised all the legislative power of the Kingdom in reference to certain permanent features of His code, and having commanded His apostles to teach all things whatsoever He had commanded them, there was no legislative power left in the Church to repeal these permanent provisions. The result is, that as to the permanent features of the code, the only powers left in the Church, are the executive and judicial.

2. The power to bind and loose was conferred upon all the apostles, and separately upon Peter, accompanied with the Keys, that symbol of supreme command.

3. What was this power to bind and loose? Was it not the power to bind and loose, by judicial decision, every member of the Church?

4. There is a plain distinction between actual infallibility and jurisdiction. The first is a qualification the second, the legal right to determine. So there is between original and final jurisdiction of the same case.

---

[1] Source: edited from a digitized copy of the original of Peter H. Burnett to Archbishop John Baptist Purcell, 22 June 1860, Archdiocese of Cincinnati Collection II-5-a, University of Notre Dame Archives.

5. It being conceded, for reasons stated at page 349 of my work, that each apostle was individually inspired, thus each possessing the qualifications of the whole combined, in what did Peter's superiority consist, if not in his superior jurisdiction?

6. If Peter possessed superior jurisdiction, not as apostle simply, but as Head of the Church, then could it have been anything else than final jurisdiction? If so, what was it?

7. If Christ created a permanent office when He made Peter supreme Head of the Church, must He not have given to each incumbent of this permanent office, the same supreme powers? In other words, if the successors of Peter possess supreme powers over all the flock, did not Peter have the same, and, as to jurisdiction, bear the same relation to the members of the Church, that all succeeding Popes have done?

8. When Christ committed His entire flock to Peter, and commanded him to confirm his brethren, did not this change include the other apostles, not only in their capacity as individuals, but in their capacity as judicial officers.

9. When our Lord said to Peter, whatsoever you shall bind or loose on earth shall be bound or loosed in heaven, did He not, by the very act, make Peter infallible in the exercise of his supreme jurisdiction over all?

10. Peter being infallible in fact, and also supreme in jurisdiction, the council of Jerusalem was but an advisory body, and could have no legal existence without him.

11. The decision of that council was attained both by the exercise of reason, and the aid of the Holy Ghost, because the Holy Spirit does not entirely supercede (*sic*) reason, but only aids it when it is insufficient of itself to reach the end aimed at. If, therefore, Peter with his advisory body, could have attained the end intended by reason alone, the aid of the Holy Ghost would not have been, in fact, given, because not required. The promise of infallible aid is a guarantee that the end shall be certainly attained. Our Lord intended to honor reason and human nature, and not to interfere, when these were already sufficient. Grace is only given in sufficient measure to enable us to discharge our duties as individuals; and the quantity must depend upon the circumstances of the case, and must be different at different times. So with official assistance. Are not these

the main reasons for calling a Council to do that which the Pope has the right to do without the Council, when, in his judgment, the occasion requires it?

12. The reason why our Lord gave superior jurisdiction to Peter over all, (the apostles included,) was because His system was permanent—the office permanent—the powers of the office always the same, and, therefore, always equally supreme over all. Had He intended His Kingdom to last only during the lives of his apostles, there could have been no reason to make Peter supreme, when all the apostles were just as certain to decide right as he himself.

These questions will present the precise point of inquiry. One of the clearest writers I have read, is Cardinal Wiseman in his Moorfield Lectures. He makes Peter superior to the other apostles in the power to bind and loose, as I understand him. Could this conceded superiority as to this power exist, except either in superior qualifications or jurisdiction, or both? As I take it, this a pretty hard question to determine. The Church, however, is amply able to determine it. Whatever the decision has been, or maybe, it must be right.

I believe I stated in my last letter, that I wished to be informed on these points, so that I might be prepared to give an exact answer, should occasion hereafter arise.

I have suffered much from neuralgia of late, but am now recovering. Give my best respects to Mr. & Mrs. Springer, & to Sister Loyola, and accept for yourself the love and dutiful submission of

Your son in Christ

Peter H Burnett

Most Rev. J. B. Purcell

1860 December 28

San Jose,

Dec. 28, 1860[1]

My dear Archbishop [Purcell],

I rec'd, a day or two since your welcome favor of the 30th Nov. but was too unwell to answer it.

I have read the works of Drs. R & K and so far as I can judge there is no great difference between us, except I agree with you that the appeal to Peter by the other Apostles was not because of ignorance in them as to matters of faith.

When I wrote you 22nd June last, I was, as I supposed, recovering; but during the months of July, August, and September I was worse off than ever. I again had an attack the 1st of this month, and am still very unwell. I can scarcely write.

I should like to visit the Atlantic States and go with you to Europe; but I am afraid it would not be a just and charitable use of money. Our dear Old Church is bleeding at every pore, and I consider it my duty, as it is my pleasure, to aid her all I can. Therefore, to expend money for my private gratification, I fear would be a sin.

My children are all grown and all married but John, who is now in Europe & Mrs. B. & myself are alone. Thirty-two years ago, we were in the same condition, with this difference; that then we beginning our married life; now we are closing up. But if my health continues bad & all medical remedies fail, you may see Mrs. B. and myself next year.

Our country is in deep peril. The real cause of our difficulties lies much deeper than most politicians are willing to admit. The institution of slavery is only the occasion seized upon to test the strength of our government. Did this cause not exist, another would. The real cause is the weakness of our system. It is beautiful in theory, but impracticable with a dense population. Virginia first defeated a

---

[1] Source: edited from a digitized copy of the original of Peter H. Burnett to Archbishop John Baptist Purcell, 28 December 1860, Archdiocese of Cincinnati Collection II-5-a, University of Notre Dame Archives.

decision of the S.C.U.S.[Supreme Court of the United States] and then Georgia did the same when Gen. Jackson was President and he submitted to it[2]. These fatal examples have been followed, until a mere mob can defeat the laws at any point, and the government has lost the confidence of legal men everywhere. It has no efficiency and no certain force.

I think Protestantism has had much to do in bringing on the present crisis. It is a restless spirit, and can only exist in strife, prejudice, & passion. The cry against Catholics had worn out, and eloquent declaimers sized upon slavery. The English Protestants have no doubt urged on the crusade. When the Union shall have been dissolved, a stronger government will become inevitable; and perhaps as a result, persecution of Catholics. We may look out for trials & sufferings. This age is material & unconscionable.

I have not seen Judge Baines work, only a few copies having been rec'd, I suppose. I trust it may do much good.

Give my very best respects to Mr. & Mrs. Springer & Sister Loyola. If you write to Bishop Wood at any time, give him my respects. I love him much.

I have read the Oct. No. of Dr. B.'s [Orestes Brownson's] Review & most of the criticisms of the C.[Catholic] press. I think the articles in that No. are erroneous in many particulars, but most of the criticisms I have read are also, and are not in the right spirit. I feel pained at the bitterness I fear is growing up between the Dr. & the editors of our papers. Difficulties must [enter] in at every step. May God help us!

Remember in yours prayers,

   Your dutiful son in Christ

   Peter H. Burnett

---

[2] In 1821 Virginia denied that the U.S. Supreme Court had appellate jurisdiction. In 1832 Supreme Court in Worcester vs. Georgia found that the State of Georgia did not have jurisdiction over the Cherokees. President Jackson did nothing to make Georgia abide by the ruling. Ed.

1861 February 9
To the Daily Alta California[1]

The Effects of Dissolution

The hour will come, and now is, when every patriot in the nation should hear the voice of his country, and they that hear should respond boldly, candidly, but kindly. To use the language of the great Pitt, upon an occasion of less importance: 'The smoothness of flattery cannot save us in this rugged crisis." There should be no abuse or flattery, either of the living or the dead; equal and exact justice should be done to all. We should refer to the facts of the past for lessons of instruction, not for bitter crimination. We must appeal to our fellow-citizens. We can not rely on politicians, whose practice it has generally been to lie against an opponent while living, and for him when gone. They have flattered us as if we were not men liable too all the infirmities belonging to the race, and have flattered one section of our common country at the expense of the other.

We are in a great crisis—a severe trial—a conclusive test; and we must meet it as best we may. If we prove unequal to the task, and cannot rise with the great occasion, then we show to the world that we are a degenerate people, and false claimants of merit not our own. Our people must think and act for their country; they should do it now. The time has been when no estimate of he value of the Union should have been made. But that time has passed. Our people, under existing circumstances, should carefully estimate the value of the Union, the cost of its dissolution, and the immediate and ultimate probable effects of that dissolution, when accomplished. When they shall have done this, they will make the greater efforts to avoid that overwhelming misfortune; for the efforts of the people, like those of an individual, will be in proportion to the estimated magnitude of the end to be attained.

It requires no argument to show the immense benefits of the Union. They are seen everywhere—on land and sea, at home and

---

[1] Published in the *Daily Alta California* of the 12th February 1861. For the date of composition see the letter of the Peter H. Burnett of 13th February 1861 to Archbishop John Baptist Purcell.

abroad. They are palpable and known to all. No people ever made more rapid progress in all the material elements of greatness. Our progress in this respect has been, perhaps, too rapid to admit of much progress in real patriotism and virtue. We have grown fat and fanatical, sectional and factious. Is this not true? But with all our faults, our country was among the first nations of the world; and in fifty years more, at the same rate of progress, she would have been *the* first in the family of nations. And now, to give up all the hopes of the great and promising future, and sink down into little petty states, the practical slaves of the great maritime powers of the world, is surely a sad termination of all our boasted pretensions.

But how can dissolution be accomplished? Only by wading through seas of blood. History records no instance of peaceful session. In the nature of thing it cannot be. Political organizations, though imperfect, are powerful. Like a tall column, the inclination of which is so great, that a touch of the finger would seem to be sufficient to overturn it, a government though weak, is still obstinate and hard to upset. It is not done without a struggle. Artificial, like natural persons, never die without the convulsive throes of death. There are inherent difficulties in the way of a dissolution of this great Union that cannot be peaceably overcome. How are we to divide the public property? Who shall keep the Navy? Who the Capital? How divide the flag of our country?—It is the most beautiful and original, in conception and design, of all the flags of earth. It is wholly unlike any other, and was made to float over a section greater than any other. Shall we tear it in twain, and give each section a part? It would then be a fit emblem of our ruined country. How are to satisfy sworn officers that hey should not execute the laws? Can we obliterate their consciences as their oaths, or have they, no consciences upon which an official oath can operate? Shall we ask them to act as if they had none? We cannot do it.

The idea of a peaceable secession is entirely erroneous. For the Government to consider it, is to plead guilty to the charge of oppresssion. It is to say, in substance, we have done wrong, and we are too mean and despicable to repair the injury. A Government cannot stultify itself in this way. If it has been unjust let it retrace its steps.

There can be no dissolution with war, and who can adequately portray the terrific horrors of such a contest? I can not, I shall not now attempt it. In the eloquent language of another, "It is the evil of which the manner is beyond discussion, and the event passes all speculation."

But the consequences of a civil war will not equal those which will flow from dissolution, when accomplished; because the former, though terrible, are transient, while the latter are permanent. Instead of distressing one or two generations, they will seriously affect the happiness of unknown millions, for ages to come.

What would be said of these evils? Let us see. We will suppose our country divided into two divisions, North and South. A glance at the map and you will see they are of a very awkward shape, both exceedingly long in proportion to their width. They are simply divided by an airline with no impenetrable mountain ranges to divide one section from the other. How can smuggling be prevented along this line? Only by having no tariff. You cannot fortify this long line, and you cannot build a Chinese wall. The people on both sided speak the same language, and the excitable masses will understand the insults of each other. How can peace be kept between populations thus situated? Will not acts of violence break out continually along this line easily passed at any point? How are the people of the great Northwest to remain satisfied with the possession of the mouths of the Mississippi by a foreign power? Though they might stand it for a time their indignation would be like a smouldering (sic) volcano, ready to break out with terrible power at any time.

Frequent wars must be the result. These wars would be carried on by regular soldiers. You cannot rely on militia men under such circumstances. Each section is threaded with railroads and telegraph lines, and any number of men could be concentrated at almost any point within three days time.

In this fast age no time is lost in sending orders, and very little in concentrating troops. Napoleon said war was the art of concentrating the greatest number of men at a given point within a given time. This is especially true at this time. The knowledge of the art of war is so equally diffused among civilized nations that numbers count, and two men will generally conquer one. Each section would be compelled to keep a large standing army, always ready to take the field. It would not do to depend on militia to repel a sudden invasion. Men engaged in the peaceful pursuit of life require time for consideration, and some discipline, before they can have confidence in each other, and courage to face a disciplined foe. The first natural impulse is to flee from danger; and men must think over it, and sleep on it, before they are prepared to meet it. The weakness of an unarmed and peaceful community was fully proven by the raid of Old John Brown.

A standing army, of reasonable size, is not an evil to be complained of; but one as large as a people can possibly maintain is a grievous burden. When this Union shall have been dissolved, each division will be compelled to keep a standing army as large as it can support. What one does the other must do. The condition of things on the Continent of Europe is proof of the correctness of these views. France has an army of seven hundred thousand men. Prussia, Russia and Austria the same, while that of England does no exceed three hundred thousand, and only some sixty thousand of these are kept at home. Were it not for colonial possessions, her standing army, in time of peace, would not exceed one hundred thousand men. The reason is that her territory cannot be invaded by land, and she has control of the sea. We are, while united, eve n in better condition, because a wide ocean lies between us and all other powerful nations. An invasion of our country united would be idle, if not impossible. But the moment we are divided, the condition of things is entirely reversed, and our enemies are at our very doors, always ready and able top attack us, and we must, of necessity, be always ready and able to meet them.

Large standing armies are not only dangerous to liberty at home, but their existence gives rise to large national debts, and most grievous taxation to pay the interest on those debts. With a divided Union, each section being invadeable by land, the credit of each would be bad, and high interest the result. England can borrow money at three percent, while France and other Powers on the Continent are compelled to pay from five to six. All the countries of Europe invadeable by land have been invaded within the last fifty years, and some of them frequently. Each successful invasion costs the country invaded about the labor of one generation, and not only destroys the ability of the nation to pay the interest upon its debts punctually, but endangers the security of the principle. People who invest their funds in government loans are generally persons who seek repose in retirement from business, and who desire a safe and certain income. If they obtain but a low rate of interest, they can manage to live within their income if the interest is certainly paid. *Security* is the great object with them.

But those are not the greatest evils that must sooner or later, flow from a severance of the Union. Republican government would not only fail on this continent, but representative government in any efficient form, could not be successfully maintained. Despotism—the one-man power—would be the legitimate and inevitable result. It would be the only practical theory under the circumstances. Government must be practical, or it fails. It may be as beautiful in theory to the imagination as the rainbow to sight, but unless strictly practical, it will not stand the storm and rigid "test of talents and of time."

The practical success of a governmental theory depends upon the circumstances and geographical position of the country governed. A form of government practical for one country, will not operate successfully in another. England, for example, not being invadeable by land can wait the sluggish movements of Parliament in making appropriations; but France, and other countries differently situated, cannot do this, especially in this fast age. When your country is invaded, and the existence of the nation is at stake, you cannot wait two months to elect a Speaker, and two months more to debate over an appropriation bill. You must have action, prompt and united, and only the strongest form of government can secure it. On the field of battle there must be but one commander-in-chief, and a country invaded is but a large battle field. Deliberative bodies are least reliable in times of extreme peril. They are then often factious or paralyzed. During the existence of the French Republic, the members of the Assembly were engaged in debating some abstract philosophical theory, while their enemies were invading France.

Our newspapers and literary writers are continually speaking in disparaging terms of the despotic governments of Europe. These objections are not thoroughly and well considered. The true fundamental cause is found in the necessities of their position. The best minds on the continent know that the English theory never can be successfully carried out, except in countries substantially situated as England is. United we are in a better condition than England, and can sustain the freest practical government in the world; and if our republican theory should fail, we can at least sustain a representative monarchy, in which the powers of government, though unlimited, are distributed among different departments which act as checks on each other.

But let us sever and divide our country, and we will be in worse condition than the people on the continent of Europe. There are many great natural features on that continent, that mark the dividing line between nations, making defense more easy, and invasion more difficult; and the doctrine of the balance of power is there established, and a weak state can exist, because the great powers will not tolerate its conquest. In our country we have no impassable mountains, and there is here no doctrine of the balance of power established, and a weak state would be at the ultimate mercy of the stronger. From the geographical features of the country, it is clear that god almighty never intended it to be divided.

It is argued by writers upon the science of government that a despotism is the strongest and most efficient. Time and commonsense has proved this to be true. In this form of government you have less security against oppression at home, and more security against oppression from abroad. What theory a people should adopt, depends upon the question, which is the greater danger? In the Revolution , our greatest danger was from abroad, and we made Washington a dictator, and by that means saved the country. If divided, the same circumstances would compel the people of different divisions to do the same thing; and as the danger would be permanent, the despotism would become so. In the wars between the little republics of South America, they confer dictatorial power on their presidents. We often blame these people as fickle; but we have not well considered the exigencies of their condition. We are fact drifting in the same direction. May we never reach the same condition.

It would seem impossible, in the nature of things, that a free press should ever exist under a despotism. The reason would seem to be, that the attacks of the press are leveled against a *single* individual. There are few individuals who would bear singly the attacks of the press, when they have the power to restrain them. It is not in human nature.

After a dissolution shall have been accomplished, the masses in every section will begin to see and understand the misfortunes of the change. We will consider ourselves degraded in our own estimation, and in that of all mankind. When one of our people travel abroad, they will ask him, "Stranger, where are you from?" "North America." (he cannot say, "The United States of America."). They will say to him, in sorrow or scorn, "You were *once* a great people." How the blush of shame will mantle his cheek! When he returns home he will speak of it to others. Our people will think and sleep upon it, brood and morn over it, until, with the energy of shame and desperation, they will rise in their might and say: "We were once great, and we will be great again, or die in the last ditch. We will prove to our children, and so the world, that we are not degenerate."

This wish will sink deep into the hearts of men, and every time a war occurs it will be uppermost in their thoughts. Years will be required to efface the recollection and love of former greatness. Every prospect of recovering it will give rise to renewed struggles.

The dissolution of our great Union is the destruction of our government on this continent. It is the most dire political evil that can befal (sic) us. Any form of government is preferable to it; because even despotism with union is better than despotism without it. We must save the Union: "It will never do to give it up so Mr. Brown."[2]

Let us all do right to the utmost of our power. Even the honest prejudices of men are entitled to respectful consideration. We may all err to some extent. If our federal theory is imperfect, let us amend it. For this purpose let us have a National Convention of our best men— our great and good men—(there must be some left yet,)—men who love justice and truth, and would not sacrifice those even to save the Union—bold, independent, yet calm, deep, thinkers, who love future more than present time—men of true greatness, who never took office for its own sake—who understand the science of government— genuine government, in the true import of the term, and who will, unhesitatingly, lay the axe to the root of evil. We are a Convention people; it is the way in which we have done things. And when we get such a Convention, let us make up our minds to ratify its labors, unless they shall be to palpably erroneous. Let us not cavil over little things. Let us exhaust every effort of conciliation and kindness before we proceed to the last resort. But if all these fail we must save the Union, if within the limits of possibility. If we have inflict punishment upon any portion of our people, let he Government inflict it with sorrow, as a father inflicts punishment upon his own child for its own good, and for the good of the family. If war cannot be avoided, then let it be conducted with dignity and unflinching firmness. And if, after

---

[2] A hackneyed phrase and refrain of the mid-nineteenth century, it generally means not to give up under trying circumstances. Ed.

all efforts, this Union must fail, then every patriot can say with Antony: "My heart is in the coffin there with Cæsar."

A TENNESSEEAN

1861 February 13

San Jose
Feby. 13, 1861[1]

Dear Archbishop, [Purcell]

I enclose to you a printed copy of my communication to the *Alta California*. I will thank you to hand it to some editor who is a friend to the sentiments expressed, and you may authorize him to say I am the author. I would send it to the *Mo. Rec.* [Metropolitan Record?] but I fear that matters will have proceeded too far before this could reach the editor to permit him to publish it. Upon an examination of it, you will find that it contains views which answer, in part, the objections urged by Protestants against the Catholic States of Europe etc. If you have read Mr. Seward's late speech, you will see a great similarity of views between us.[2] This is entirely accidental. My communication was written and mailed on the 9th Inst. and appeared in the *Alta [California]* on the 12th and the speech of Mr. Seward first appeared in this State in the *Sacramento Union* of 11th and did not reach me at this place until the 12th at about 5 P.M. When I read Mr. Seward's speech, I was struck with the similarity of our views upon the evils of dissolution.

There are several typographical errors in the com [communication]: which I have corrected, and I have stricken out one line in deference to the opinion of others. One of the serious maxims

---

[1] Source: edited from a digitized copy of the original of Peter H. Burnett to Archbishop John Baptist Purcell, 13 February 1861, Archdiocese of Cincinnati Collection II-5-a, University of Notre Dame Archives.

[2] Mr. Seward, who in January 1861 accepted the position of Secretary of State in Lincoln's cabinet, gave a speech in Baltimore suggesting a compromise on slavery that aimed at preserving the Union. Ed.

of my life has been the saying: "It will never do to give it up so, Mr Brown."[3] I owe my success to it.

Pray for me and mine

Yours most dutifully

Peter H. Burnett

---

[3] A hackneyed phrase and refrain of the mid-nineteenth century, it generally means not to give up under trying circumstances. Ed.

1862 July 16

San Jose, Cal.[1]

July 16, 1862.

My Dear Sir—

A mutual friend has sent me your card announcing yourself a candidate for Congress. I hope you may be elected. I only wish I had it in my power to vote for you. I would do so with great pleasure. I see you are for the Union. So am I to the last extent. While I indulge no bitterness of feeling, and look with sorrow, and regret upon the rebellion, I am fully convinced that a permanent dissolution of the Union would be comparative ruin to us all. Our greatness, our peace, our freedom, and our prosperity would be gone. Despotism, inevitable despotism, would be the <u>ultimate and legitimate result</u> of disunion. This must be plain to the statesman. In the very nature of things it could not be otherwise.

I never expected to live to see my country involved in a civil war. God forbid that I should live to see to see it again so involved. I sincerely love peace; but I can not possibly see how the Federal Government could have avoided a resort to force. The severed states assumed to go out upon two main grounds: 1. That secession was a <u>constitutional</u> right. 2. That....

...rare send another. It is at your disposal Aug. 11, 1862.

P.H.B.

---

[1] Source: c970 f104. From a photocopy of the original by permission of The University of Missouri, Western Historical Manuscript Collection—Columbia, MO.

Part 8

Bank President 1862-1880

1873 February 18

Pacific Bank [Letter Head][1]

Cor. Pine & Sansome Sts. [Letter Head]

San Francisco Cal. [Letter Head]

Feby. 13 1873

Dear Cousin–

I have just seen Linsay Marshall who informs me that you had moved to Franklin County Mo.

Hearing from you has revived old recollections; and though I cannot write with the same ease I once could, I determined I would write you a short letter.

I am president of this Bank and have been since 1863. We are all well and getting along safely. Mrs. Ryland has 9 living children, Dwight 5, Romie 6, and John 5—in all 25. Two of the grand daughters are grown; namely Adele Ryland and Harriet M. Burnett. Armstead died May 25th 1862 and Sallie May 24th 1861. Both died of consumption

Please write me and give me a history of yourself and family and of the kin in your state.

Give my warmest love to all the kin

      Yours truly

      P. H. Burnett

---

[1] Source: c3655 f38. From a photocopy of the original by permission of the University of Missouri, Western Historical Manuscript Collection—Columbia, MO.

1873 March 19

Peter H. Burnett, President Orlando H. Bogart, Cashier[Letterhead]

Recd. Mar 25, 1873 [Handwrtten]

Pacific Bank San Francisco Cal [letterhead][1]

March 19th 1873

Dear Cousin Glen—

Your most welcome favor of the 11th Inst. came duly to hand yesterday. Madam B. read it with much pleasure. You were always esteemed by her.

As I write with more labor than I did years ago, I will proceed with a history of the family.

Dwight resides in this city—has 5 living children Hattie 19, George 17, Frank 15, Romie 10, and Ruby 3.

Letitia still lives in San Jose and has 9 living children—Ada 21, John N. 18, Norma 14, Frank 12, Joseph 10, Hattie 8, Jacitus 5, Charles 6, and Dwight 3.

Romie lives in this city and has 6 living children. Richard 19, Ryland 17, Addie 15, William 12, Belle 8 and Margaret 4.

John M. Burnett lives in this city and has 5 living children—Mira 9, Sallie 7, Margaritta 5, Peter 3 and David 1½.

I am now 65 Mrs. B 61. Ryland is about 44, Wallace 43, Dwight 43, Letitia 40, Romie 37, and John 34. Their wives are all younger than they are. Mr. Ryland has been a banker with M. McLaughlin at San Jose for more than 3 years. Wallace is now Chief Justice on the State supreme court. Dwight is at present out of business and John is a lawyer getting into a good practice. All our children and grand children are satisfactory to us. We are happy. We look forward with hope to the end of life and trust we shall be saved in Heaven. Our toils will soon be over. Death is the end of suffering and the beginning of joy.

---

[1] Source: c 3655 f38. From a photocopy of the original by permission of The University of Missouri, Western Historical Manuscript Collection—Columbia, MO.

Brother Glen came to Cal. in 1855 and returned to Oregon 1856—moved again to Cal. in about 1866 and returned to Oregon again in May 1871, and is there now, but I hear he intends moving again to Cal this spring. All his children are grown except John, Albert and Annie who are with him yet. Albert and Annie are twins about 15. John is about 17. Glen has 9 children living—Martha, Mary, Lirvis, Peter, Hanny, Matthew, John, Albert and Annie. Martha, Mary, Hanny and Peter are married and the two first have children grown. Glen has six grand children married and several great grand children.

Brother Wm. still lives in Oregon in the old place selected in 1847, and has 4 children living—3 married daughters and one unmarried son, and several grand children.

Brother White lives in Oregon and has about 8 children the oldest about grown.

Brother Thomas lives in Salinas City the new County Seat of Monterey Co. Cal. and has some 5 children. Two of his daughters are grown—one of them is married.

Glen is an Elder in the Campbellite Church and Thomas is a Methodist Preacher South.

Old man Ricketts died a few years after you left. He had an operation performed on the tumor on his neck and died from the effects of the operation. His daughter Harriet and Barrons married away and I have lost the track of him. I never saw Harriet's husband.

I should have been glad had you settled in this state. Still I could not advise any to sell out in MO. and move here unless he had very large capital as real estate is too high for it to be profitable. Farming in Cal. is more pleasant than profitable. Yet many do well and many fail.

Give my kindest love to your wife to Cousin Leann and family. You did not give me the name of the lady you married etc.

Write me again. I would like so much to receive a letter from Cousin Leann.

                Your Cousin

                Peter H. Burnet

Part 9
Author, Retiree 1880-1895

1883 May 21

San Francisco,[1]

610 Jones Street

May 21, 1883

Dear Paxton,

Your kind letter of the 14th came to hand this morning.

I am glad to hear that my book gave you and your family, and Mrs. Cole warm satisfaction. It was written with a kind and generous intent.

The "Old Pioneer" cost for the first 1000 copies about $860. The Appletons do their work well, but their charges are higher in consequence. I preferred having the work published in N.Y. because they could give it a wider circulation than a local publisher, so many of my acquaintances living East.

I did not mention the nature of the work I am engaged upon, because it is doubtful whether I will live to finish it, and because I did not wish it known to the public. My rule is never, except upon rare occasions, to subscribe for a work, and I never publish a work by subscription as I desire to let it rest solely upon its merits, and never wish to excite expectations by letting it be known that I intend to publish a work until it is out for all to see and judge. But I will tell you <u>in confidence</u> that it is a work upon the truth of our common Religion. If I am still spared some 18 months longer in fair health, I think I will have it finished, and I may publish it or leave it behind me in manuscript. Of course, I do not expect to make any money by the work, as that is not my object, but to save souls. It is the clear duty of every man to do all the good he can <u>reasonably</u> do, and to be prepared and willing to go at any time and in any manner our Father may choose. I am waiting in faith, hope, and charity for the summons. All I can say is "God's will be done."

---

[1] Source: c1025 f33. From a photocopy of the original by permission of The University of Missouri, Western Historical Manuscript Collection—Columbia, MO.

I should like to see you very much. No doubt we could spend many happy hours together. We have been very much blessed, and should be very grateful. This is a time for all to do their duty.

I am truly sorry to hear of the condition of the old acquaintance whose name you mention.

I forgot to state that my work was stereotyped. What the plates cost I cannot say. If you simply publish a stated no. of copies it will cost less, but then you cannot publish any more unless you have your work stereotyped.

All my family are in usual health except one granddaughter about 7 years old, and she is not dangerous. My sister is now with her son-in-law, Mr. Wigler at Cloverdale, Cal. some 65 miles from this city.[2] She left my home early in April. I have heard from her lately. They are all well. Her youngest child Harry Cain was married to Della Parlin at Los Angeles Dec. 20, 1882. He is an excellent man and she is worthy of him.

Give my kindest regards to your good family, and write me when you can.

Your Old Friend

Peter H. Burnett

---

[2] Sister Elizabeth Ann

1885 March 11

A communication to a family member:[1]

As relates to myself, I must refer you to the "Old pioneer" [*Recollections and Opinions of an Old Pioneer*] for events which occurred up to the last date of that narrative, 6 Sept. 1878. I will mention a few circumstances happening since that date. On 12 January, 1880, I ceased to be president of the Pacific Bank (having reached the age of 72) and retired to private life. During the years 1880-1-2 and 3 and one half of 1884, I was incessantly employed in the composition and publication of my late work, "Reasons why we should believe in God, love God," lately issued from the press of the Catholic Publication Society Co., 9 Barelay [Barclay] St., N.Y. City.

After keeping house for about fifty-five years, I closed out in September last; when I had finished my work, and was very much exhausted and reduced and needed rest. I have since spent my time with my children and am at last permanently located with my son, John M. Burnet, my youngest living child. Having invested all my little capital in United States Bonds, I have no business cares, and while my income is moderate, it is ample for my reasonable wants with some to spare. I live in plain but comfortable style, my life is private, tranquil and happy, and I spend my time in peaceful, hopeful, preparation for death. My four children and thirty grandchildren are all within two hours travel by rail. So far as I can see, my work is substantially finished and I wait with patience and resignation, the call of the great teacher, Death.

---

[1] http://www-personal.umich.edu/~cgaunt/etc/v99i31.txt. 2011/12/19. "From Peter H. Burnet himself, 11 March 1885."

1888 September 17

San Francisco[1]

1713 Larkin Street

Sep. 17, 1888

Dear Cousin Glen—

Your welcome letter came duly to hand.

Since you left we have had two severe cases of sickness.

Frank O Ryland, second son of C. T. Ryland, and a most noble young man, was taken with hemorrhage from the throat and lungs about 6 or 8 weeks ago. He is now 27 years of age, and has been in the Commercial Bank of San Jose some 5 years, and was Cashier at the time. He and his eldest sister, Ada, started by rail to Lake Tahoe; and when they reached Auburn station this side of the Summit, he was so sick that they were forced to give up the remainder of the journey. After remaining in Auburn some time they finally brought him home, where he is now finally recovering.

Some two or three weeks later William T Wallace, third son of Judge Wallace, was taken with the same disease. He is 29, and is a young lawyer residing in Martinez, about 30 miles from here. They brought him home where he now lies very sick. There are some hopes of his recovery, but his symptoms are bad. He and Frank Ryland are both tall and slender and rather delicate in constitution. Their mothers have been much distressed over their conditions.

I am much pleased with the information contained in your most welcome letter. I have a bundle of letters labelled, (sic) "Family History," and will place your letter among the others.

All the rest of the kin are well. My own health is fair.

---

[1] Source: c3655 f42. From a photocopy of the original by permission of The University of Missouri, Western Historical Manuscript Collection—Columbia, MO.

My brother Glen's widow has had another attack, but had about recovered a few days ago. She is the last of 5 brothers and 3 sisters, and is about 73.

Let me hear from you from time to time. We all esteem and love you, and all will welcome your letters. Give my love to your wife and family.

May God bless you and yours!

> Your Cousin
> Peter H. Burnett

AUTHOR, RETIREE

1889

Preface [1]

The discovery of gold in California in the month of January, 1848, while the country was in the military possession of the United States, led to a state of things—social, financial and literary —never before witnessed in the world; and which it is safe to predict will never occur again. There being no prohibitory legislation, the mines were thrown open to all the world upon equal terms. This privilege, the richness of the mines themselves, and the ease and quick success with which they were at first worked, caused the sudden assemblage of great numbers of young men from every part of the civilized world. With very rare exceptions, they came simply as eager seekers of gold, with no intention of remaining permanently in the country, but only first to accumulate, then to return and enjoy. As they came to acquire, not to invest capital in California, they had about an equal start, as every sane and healthy adult could readily find employment at a renumerative (sic) compensation. In those early days the whole community substantially lived under the theory of an equal and ample division of property.

One of the marked incidents accompanying the early golden days of California, was the almost entire suspension of the literary ability, and especially of the poetic talent of our people. A glance over the files of the papers published in California previous to 1856, will show, I think, how few and brief were the local poetic productions of the time. While I was in the mines in the months of November and December, 1848, "I became acquainted with John C. McPherson, a young genial spirit from old Scotland. He was a generous soul and cared little for wealth. On Christmas Eve he composed a very pretty song, beginning 'Yuba, dear Yuba.' * * * No one then in the mines except McPherson had poetic fire enough in his soul to write a song."

---

[1] Peter H. Burnett, Preface, *A Chaplet of Verse: by California Catholic Writers*, eds. D. O. Crowley and Charles Anthony Doyle (San Francisco: Diepenbrock & Co. 1889).

But the great Pacific Coast is the natural home of the scholar, the novelist and the poet. It lies upon the mildest and grandest ocean in the world, and possesses a scenery and climate unsurpassed. These must, in due course of time, produce writers of the first class. Even at this comparatively early day, many creditable productions have flowed from the pens of our authors.

The following selection of poems is made from the compositions of different local writers, several of whom are natives of California. The main purpose of the publication is to aid that most practical and deserving charity, "The Youths' Directory."

By an Act approved March 25, 1880, the State of California furnishes pecuniary aid to "each and every institution in this State conducted for the support and maintenance of minor orphans, half orphans, or abandoned children," for such orphans, half orphans and abandoned children, not over fourteen years of age, as may be supported and maintained by such institution. The same allowance is made to cities, counties and towns for like services.

While the terms abandoned children may be difficult to define with exact certainity (sic), they would hardly include the cases of those children whose parents do all in their power to support and maintain them but are unable to do so from sickness or other misfortune.

The Youths' Directory is not an asylum where "orphans, half orphans and abandoned children" are continuously supported and maintained in one place until they reach a certain age, but it is a peculiar institution mainly intended for the protection of a different class of boys; who, while their condition is about as bad as that of "orphans, half orphans and abandoned children," are not entitled to any aid from the State; for I am informed upon good authority, that "this institution does not now receive, and never has received State aid of any kind," but depended entirely upon private contributions for its support.

The chief purpose of this noble society is the protection of homeless boys, whose parents, from sickness or other misfortune, are unable to support and maintain them. Such boys are provided by the Directory with a home and support until they can be placed with good families as apprentices to learn some honest and useful occupation, or until they are otherwise provided for.

As these little and helpless unfortunates are not the authors of their unhappy condition, they are, for that reason, the more deserving of our warmest sympathy and support.

Peter H. Burnett.

1890 October 6

San Francisco, Cal[1]

1713 Larkin Street,

October 6, 1890

David W. May

My Dear Nephew

Your kind and most welcome letter was received a few days since.

I quit the Pacific Bank in January 1880, and since then I have lived in great privacy. Having invested my little capital in U.S. 4 per cent Bonds, I have a moderate but certain income. My wife died in September 1879. I have lived with my son, John M. Burnett, since February 7, 1885, and give my time mainly to a calm and earnest preparation for death.

I have two sons, Dwight J. and John M. and two daughters, Mrs. L. M. Ryland and Mrs. R. J. Wallace still living. I have twenty seven grandchildren and seven great-grandchildren living. They all live in California, a majority of them in this city.

Give my love to your Mother whom I remember to have seen in 1866. Also to all the relatives. All our kin in this vicinity are as well as usual.

Now, my Dear Nephew, as I write with great labor, you must write several letters to my one and give me the ages etc. of your family etc. I will be glad to hear from you. I love my kin. I must say they are worthy. God bless You!

Your Old Uncle
Peter H. Burnett

---

[1] Source: c1483. From a photocopy of the original by permission of the University of Missouri, Western Historical Manuscript Collection—Columbia, MO.

AUTHOR, RETIREE

1891 May 21

May 21 1891[1]

Dear Nephew—

Your welcome letter of April 27 came duly to hand. I am glad to hear from you at any and all times, and I am pleased that you do not count letters with me.

I write with great labor and must beg you to excuse this short letter. Let me hear from you at intervals, I can read without labor.

Give my love to your Mother and all the kin

Your Old Uncle
Peter H. Burnett

---

[1] Source: c1483 From a photocopy of the original by permission of the University of Missouri, Western Historical Manuscript Collection—Columbia, MO.

Appendix

EXHIBIT A: THE INAUGURAL ADDRESS 1849

THE INAUGURAL ADDRESS
Of

Peter Burnett

1st Civil Governor of California, Independent Democrat

Presented: December 20, 1849

GENTLEMEN OF THE SENATE AND ASSEMBLY: The circumstances under which you have assembled are most new, interesting, and extraordinary—demanding our devout gratitude to the Supreme Being, the Creator and Father of us all.

You compose the first Legislature of the first free American State organized upon the distant shores of the Pacific. How rapid, astonishing, and unexampled have been the changes in California! Twenty months ago California was inhabited by a sparse populations pastoral people—deriving their main sustenance from their flocks and herds, and a scanty cultivation of the soil—their trade and business limited, and their principal exports consisting of hides and tallow. Within that short period has been made the discovery of the rich, extensive, and exhaustless gold mines of California; and how great already have been its effects! The trade and business of the country have been. revolutionized and reversed—the population increased beyond all expectation—commerce extended—our ports filled with shipping from every nation and clime—our commercial cities have sprung up as if by enchantment—our beautiful bays and placid streams now navigated by the power of steam: and amidst all this unprecedented bustle and excitement, the energetic, intrepid, and sensible people of California have framed a constitution for our new State—the Pacific Star.

You have assembled as the representatives of the people to put the State Government into practical operation; and the duty you have before you is a sublime but difficult task, requiring great unanimity, vigor, and wisdom in your councils.

APPENDIX

The first question you have to determine is, whether you will proceed at once with the general business of legislation, or await the action of Congress upon the question of our admission into the Union. The convention which formed the Constitution under which you have assembled, and the people who have ratified it with so great unanimity, have settled that question for themselves; but they have not settled it for you or for me. The same oath that you and I have taken to support the Constitution of California, also obliges us to support the Constitution of the United States; and when the provisions of the two instruments conflict, the Constitution of our common country must prevail. That great instrument which now governs more than twenty millions of inhabitants, and links in one common destiny thirty States, and is to govern the hundred millions that will soon succeed us, and the many free States yet to be, must claim our purest affections, and our first and highest duty. If, then, it would be inconsistent with the just rights of the United States, for you to proceed to put the state government into full operation, before she be formally admitted into the Union, you should, without hesitation, forbear, and leave our people still to suffer on, rather than violate one single principle of the great fundamental law of the land.

But I apprehend there can exist no well founded objection to the proposition, that you have the right to proceed at once to put the State machine into full and practical operation. The Federal Government is one of LIMITED, DELEGATED POWERS, and although supreme within its appropriate sphere, yet outside that sphere, and in reference to the reserved powers of the States or the people, it has nothing to do. So far as their reserved powers are concerned, the States are independent of the general government, of each other, and of the whole world. The exercise of the powers conferred by the Constitution of California can in no way interfere with the rights of the United States, as they only assume to regulate our own internal, social, and business relations with each other.

Perhaps it may be satisfactory to refer to a few examples to be found in the Constitutions of some of the new States. In the Constitution of Missouri, adopted on the nineteenth day of July, eighteen hundred and twenty, there is a provision that an election shall be held throughout the State, on the fourth Monday of August of the same year, for a Governor, Lieutenant Governor, Member of Congress, Members of the Legislature, and other officers. The Legislature were required to meet on the third Monday of September, and to pass laws of a permanent character, at their first session. It is well known that the state was not admitted into the Union upon her first application; but in the meantime, so far as I am enabled to state from information, having no access to the records of the state, the state government was put into successful operation. Her Members of Congress were not permitted to take their seats, and she was excluded from all voice in the National Legislature; but so far as her mere internal regulations were concerned she had the same rights BEFORE that she had AFTER her admission.

In the Constitution of Michigan, adopted in convention, begun and held on the 11th day of May, 1835, it is provided that an election be held for Governor, Lieutenant Governor, members of the Legislature, and a representative in Congress, on the first Monday of October, of the same year, and the first meeting of the Legislature was held on the first Monday of November, 1835. In that year Congress was not in session after the 4th day of March until the first Monday of December following, so that the state government of Michigan was in full operation before application could be made to Congress for her admission into the Union.

These reasons and precedents would seem to leave no doubt of your right to proceed at once with the great business of Legislation, so imperiously demanded by the destitute and confused condition of the country; and I would therefore most earnestly recommend you to set about the great and difficult task before you, without hesitation or delay.

Among the first and most important of your duties, besides the local legislation necessary for the state, will be the adoption of a civil and criminal code of law for her government. This is an object of supreme importance; and it is the more so from the consideration that the action of the first Legislature will hardly be disturbed by any succeeding one. What shall be done now cannot be touched or changed HEREAFTER, but at great cost and inconvenience. The new State of California is now in a position to adopt the most improved and enlightened code of law to be found in any of the States. The science of law is not yet fully perfected, and admits of some improvement, and in our new position we can readily adopt all the improvements that the researches and experience of others have made. I have given the subject my most careful attention for some years past; and as the result of my own convictions, I recommend the

APPENDIX

adoption of the following codes, so far as they are applicable to the condition of the State, and not modified by the Constitution or the acts of the Legislature.

1. The definition of crimes and misdemeanors contained in the Common Law of England.

2. The English Law of Evidence.

3. The English Commercial Law.

4. The Civil Code of the State of Louisiana.

5. The Louisiana Code of Practice.

These codes, it is thought, would combine the best features of both the civil and the common law, and at the same time omit the most objectionable portions of each. The civil code of Louisiana was compiled by the most able of American jurists – contains the most extensive and valuable references to authorities – has undergone no material changes for the last twenty years – and for its simplicity, brevity, beauty, accuracy, and equity, is perhaps unequalled.

Its provisions almost entirely relate to general subjects, not local, and would be quite applicable to the condition and circumstances of the State. The civil law, the basis of the Louisiana civil code, aside from its mere political maxims, and so far only as it assumes to regulate the intercourse of men with each other, is a system of the most refined, enlarged, and enlightened principles of equity and justice. So great a portion of the cases that will arise in our courts, for some years to come, must be decided by the principles of the civil law, that the study of its leading features will be forced upon our judges and members of the bar. The civil code of Louisiana being a mere condensation of the most valuable portions of the civil law, would greatly lessen the labors of our jurists and practitioners; and from the simplicity and yet comprehensive nature of its provisions, a general knowledge of the leading principles of the law might the more readily be diffused among the people. A sufficient number of copies of both the civil code and the code of practice could be procured in New Orleans at a much less cost than they could be published here.

The grave and delicate subject of revenue is one to which I would call your particular attention. From the best estimate I have been enabled to make, the current expenses of the State Government for the first year will reach half a million of dollars; but most probably will exceed that sum. This large amount can be raised only in two modes – either by loan or by taxation. The first of these modes is objectionable on many accounts. The high rate of interest, which money so readily commands in the markets of California, would prevent the State from negotiating a loan, except at such exorbitant rates as would be ruinous to her future prosperity. There can be no policy, perhaps, more injurious to our young State, before her credit is established or her resources developed, than that system of borrowing which has proved so disastrous to so many new States. As between individuals, it is exceedingly doubtful whether the credit system, upon the whole, has produced most good or most evil; and the objection applies, with much greater force, to organized States or communities. There is something wrong in principle in the very idea of entailing our burdens upon posterity. When a State borrows money to construct some great and permanent improvement, and leaves future generations to pay the debt, she also leaves them the work itself, as some sort of compensation. The violation of principle consists in the PRESENT generation assuming to act for and to bind the next without their consent. But the case is still worse, when a State borrows money to defray the ordinary expenses of her civil administration; because she bequeaths a debt to posterity, without any means to pay it. It would be similar to the case of a father borrowing money for his own purposes during his life, and expending the same upon objects transitory in their character, and, when he makes his will, to put in a clause that his children shall pay the debt, while, at the same time, he leaves them nothing to pay with.

The only available and just mode of procuring the indispensable means of supporting the State government is by a system of direct taxation: the most fair, simple, and just mode of taxation ever resorted to. The people then know distinctly what the blessings of government cost them, and which is the more desirable, a plain republican government, administered upon economical principles, or a more extravagant system of expenditure; and, if they should not be willing to pay enough to carry on an economical government, it would at once solve the great problem whether they are capable of self-government or not. The people of California may be safely trusted upon this subject; for there are no people more able and willing to pay the just taxes necessary to support the government than they. What property they have commands a high and ready price, paid in the precious metals; and labor meets such ample reward, that no healthy man can complain of poverty. The law protects every man in his person and property. For the protection it gives his person he ought to pay a capitation or poll tax; and for the protection it gives his property, he ought of right to pay a tax in proportion to its amount and value.

I recommend, therefore, the imposition of a poll tax, and a tax upon real and personal property in proportion to its value. I also recommend that provisions be made that no individual who shall refuse to pay his taxes, being able, when they shall be legally demanded, shall be permitted to bring a civil suit in any court in this State for the period of one year, and not then until all arrearages are paid. This may seem a harsh measure, but it is not. The honest individual who pays his taxes will not feel it, and he who wishes to evade the payment of the just dues of the State, OUGHT TO FEEL IT. There are some individuals in California who intend to remain here only while they extract her gold, and enjoy the protection of her laws, and who would willingly return without paying anything. This is particularly the case with respect to the great mass of foreigners in the country. In remote sections of the State it may be very difficult to enforce the collection of the revenue by levy and sale. Many individuals, perfectly able to pay, would find means to avoid the collector. But the silent and sure operation of the provision I recommend would insure the collection of the revenue promptly, and with but little expense. There are few men who would, by their OWN VOLUNTARY ACT, exclude themselves from the courts of justice.

I recommend that the collectors be authorized to receive the taxes in California gold, at the usual rate of sixteen dollars per ounce Troy.

Were the State revenue to be collected in coin it would greatly increase the demand already so great for the Custom House, and would thus operate still more injuriously upon the laboring miner: besides, it would be almost impossible for persons in the mines to provide themselves with the coin. I would also recommend that the revenue law be so framed as to require the Collector to go around with the Assessor; otherwise one half the revenue, in some districts, would be lost, in consequence of the frequent change of residence.

The operation of a reasonable and sound system of taxation upon the agricultural resources of the country would be most decidedly beneficial in a very short period. Most of the fine agricultural lands of California are now in the hands of a few persons, who suffer them to remain wild and uncultivated. A few months ago, when the population was small, and the wants of the community few and simple, the natural pasturage of the country, with a limited cultivation of the soil, was ample for all the purposes of life; but, under the changed circumstances, when our country teems with people who must be fed, and when the population is so rapidly augmenting, it is unreasonable, if not impossible, that the country should remain in a state of nature.

No country can safely depend upon an uncertain foreign supply of the first necessaries of life. Such a supply would be subject to all the vicissitudes of war or peace, would never be regular, and prices would always be fluctuating, either extravagantly high, or so low as to discourage importation. The provisions themselves are generally stale and unwholesome, and, no doubt, one half the disease suffered in the country has arisen from this prolific source. When those who own such immense tracts of rich, fertile, and beautiful lands, now in a state of nature, producing no rents or profits, shall have to pay taxes upon them in proportion to their value, they will find it their interest to sell out portions to those who will cultivate them; thus encouraging the agricultural industry of the country, and, at the same time, greatly increasing the value of the portions not sold. In the last fifteen months the number of cattle in the country has been rapidly decreasing, while population has increased in the same ratio. Fresh meats are indispensable to our health, and cannot be imported; and, if this state of things should continue only a few years longer, the increased expense of living will be so great that mining and other kinds of business must cease to be profitable. The Constitution makes it the duty of the Legislature to encourage agriculture—that first and noblest of all industrial pursuits; but I am not aware of any other means, at present, within your power than those I have suggested.

That portion of our people resident in California before its cession to the United States, have not been accustomed to a system of direct taxation; and being the principal owners of the landed property of the country, may not at first understand the justice or necessity of the revenue system our Constitution and condition make it indispensable for you to adopt. The Mexican government derived no revenue from California, except that produced by a high tariff upon imports. These taxes were paid by the people in the shape of extravagant prices for the merchandise they purchased. But this portion of our people will soon learn that, under our system, the federal government can alone levy duties upon imports—that the State cannot do so, and has only left to her a resort to a system of direct taxation to raise those means indispensable to the very existence of the government itself. They will also see that our Constitution establishes the just principle that all property shall be taxed in proportion to its value; and that the Legislature has no power or right either to favor or oppress any class of persons, but must look to the property itself, in whose hands so ever it may be found. They will also learn that the same American manufactures, upon which they were accustomed to pay such high duties, now come into our ports duty free, and that they are compensated for the direct taxes they pay in the increased value of their property, and the decreased prices of the merchandise they consume.

It has been as truly as beautifully said, that a wise legislator adapts his action to circumstances. These he cannot create or remove, he can only conform to things he cannot control. He must take mankind and society as he finds them, not as he would make them. He may so shape his laws as to produce a gradual improvement, but he cannot at once to reverse or overcome even the prejudices of a community.

Our Constitution has wisely prohibited slavery within the State; so that the people of California are once and forever free from this great social and political evil. But the Constitution has made no provision in reference to the settlement of free people of color within our limits, but has left the Legislature to adopt such legislation upon this delicate and important subject, as may be deemed most essential to the happiness of our people. The Constitution excludes this class of persons from the right of suffrage, and from all offices of honor or profit under the State.

For some years past I have given this subject my most serious and candid attention; and I most cheerfully lay before you the result of my own reflections. There is, in my opinion, but one of two consistent courses to take in reference to this class of population; either to admit them to the full and free enjoyment of all the privileges guaranteed by the Constitution to others, or exclude them from the State. If we permit them to settle in our State, under existing circumstances, we consign them, by our own institutions, and the usages of our own society, to a subordinate and degraded position, which is in itself but a species of slavery. They would be placed in a situation where they would have no efficient motives for moral or intellectual improvement, but must remain in our midst, sensible of their degradation, unhappy themselves, enemies to the institutions and the society whose usages have placed them there, and forever fit teachers in all the schools of ignorance, vice, and idleness.

Our position upon the Pacific, our commercial and mineral attractions, would bring swarms of this population to our shores. Already we have almost every variety of the human race among us—a heterogeneous mass of human beings, of every language and of every hue. That period is rapidly approaching, when the natural increase of population in the States east of the Rocky Mountains will render Slave labor of little or no value, and when investments in that species of property will cease to be remunerative. If measures are not early taken by this State, slaves will be manumitted in the slave States, and contracts made with them to labor as hirelings for a given number of years, and they will be brought to California in great numbers. Our State is now in a position to take an efficient stand upon the subject. A few years delay will make it almost, if not quite, impossible, to do that which can be so easily accomplished now. If California will take a decided stand now, and firmly maintain it, a few years' experience will demonstrate the practical utility of the measure. That weak and sickly sympathy, that misplaced mercy, that would hesitate to adopt a salutary measure today, but would suffer all the inevitable consequences of tomorrow, may consider the policy I propose as harsh in its character; but if it is calculated to produce the greatest good to the greatest number, it is the best humanity. It could be no favor, and no kindness, to permit that class of population to settle in the State under such humiliating conditions, although they might think otherwise; while it would be a most serious injury to us. We have certainly the right to prevent any class of population from settling in our State, that we may deem injurious to our society. Had they been born here, and had acquired rights in consequence, I should not recommend any measure to expel them. They are not now here, except a few in comparison with the numbers that would be here; and the object is to keep them out. I therefore call your most serious attention to this subject, believing it to be one of the first importance.

The Constitution provides that the sessions of the Legislature shall be annual on the first Monday of January. It also provides that the members of the Legislature shall be chosen on the Tuesday next after the first Monday in November, unless otherwise ordered by the

APPENDIX

Legislature. The Legislature at its first session is required to appoint a Comptroller Treasurer, Attorney General, Surveyor General, three Justices of the Supreme Court, and Judges of the District Courts; but Judges of the County Courts, Clerk of the Supreme Court, District Attorneys, Sheriffs, Coroners, Assessors, Collectors, Justices of the Peace, and other officers, must be elected by the people.

These officers are most important, and the government cannot be put into operation without them. The question then arises, will the Legislature provision for the election of these officers at as early a day as practicable, or shall their election be deferred to the general election in November next? I would most respectfully recommend that a general election be held throughout the State for these officers at the earliest convenient period.

It will be necessary to pass a general act in reference to the Judiciary. I recommend that a criminal court be established for the city of San Francisco, and also one for the city of Sacramento. The business of these cities is so great that it becomes necessary to separate the civil and criminal jurisdiction, and place them in separate and distinct courts.

I would call your attention to the thirty-seventh section of the fourth Article, and to the fourth section of the eleventh Article of the Constitution, having reference to the "organization of cities and incorporated villages," and the establishing "a system of county and town governments throughout the State." The objects contemplated in these two sections are very important to the peace, beauty, and health of our commercial cities. Great distress and inconvenience have already been experienced by the inhabitants of our growing towns for want of some efficient system of city government; and until some general and comprehensive system can be adopted, applicable to all places in the State having a certain number of inhabitants, there will be no permanent improvement in the present unfortunate condition of things.

I have now suggested to you, gentlemen, such of the more important measures I have thought it my duty to recommend, and the limits of a message would allow; but there are many other and important subjects to which only a very brief allusion can be made. It will be necessary to pass an act in reference to crimes and misdemeanors, affixing such punishment to each as may be in just proportion to the offence, and in the power of the State to inflict, under existing circumstances. It would also be highly useful to pass an act to prevent the desertion of seamen from merchant vessels visiting our ports. By the laws of all civilized countries the contracts of seamen are regarded as sacred, and are therefore rigidly and specially enforced.

I would also recommend the establishment of an inspection for provisions at San Francisco, that our people may not hereafter suffer so great losses from the purchase of injured or spoiled provisions.

It will be necessary to divide the State into counties to determine the number of justices of the peace, to make provision for the acknowledgment and registration of deeds and the registration of the separate property of the wife, and to protect from forced sale a certain portion of the homestead and other property, of all heads of families. It will also be necessary to make provision for the early construction of suitable public buildings, such as will answer for the present purposes, and may be useful for public offices hereafter.

You have before you a great amount of labor, and you will have to assume great and weighty responsibilities. The first legislators of a new State, under ordinary circumstances, have a difficult duty to discharge. But our position upon the Pacific ocean, the relation we bear to the other States of the Union, and to the civilized and semi-civilized world, impose upon us peculiar responsibilities. We have to develop the great resources of our new country. Our commercial advantages are greater than our mineral, great as these are. The latter will supply as the necessary capital to build our commercial cities and to carry on the most extended commerce. We shall soon be in close commercial intercourse with the teeming population of the old world. The rich and cheap productions of Asia are already pouring into our ports, and a few years will give us the wholesale trade of the entire Northwest coast. We have a new community to organize—a new State to build up. We have also to create and sustain a reputation in the face of the misconceptions of our character that are entertained elsewhere. But we have the most ample and the most excellent materials out of which to construct a great community and a great State. The emigration to this country from the States east of the Rocky Mountains, consists of their most energetic, enterprising, and intelligent population; while the timid and the idle, who had neither the energy nor the means to get here, were left to remain at home.

APPENDIX

Either a brilliant destiny awaits California or one the most sordid and degraded. She will be marked by strong and decided characteristics. Much will depend upon her early legislation. To confine her expenditures within due bounds, to keep the young State out of debt, and to make her punctual and just in all her engagements, are some of the sure and certain means to advance and secure her prosperity. I hope we may be able to build up for her a reputation that will bear the just criticisms of the sensible, fair, and candid of all parties, as well as the vindictive assaults of her enemies, and the errors and indiscretions of her friends. In all your efforts to accomplish this great object, you may depend upon my most cordial co-operation in all such measures as I can conscientiously approve. And now relying with sincere but humble confidence upon the favor and the protection of the Supreme Ruler, who governs nations as well as individuals, I subscribe myself,

Your fellow-citizen,

Peter H. Burnett.

EXHIBIT B: THE GOVERNOR'S MESSAGE 1851

THE GOVERNOR'S MESSAGE
Peter Burnett

Presented: January 6 1851

GENTLEMEN OF THE SENATE AND ASSEMBLY:

Since the adjournment of the Legislature we have passed through many scenes, some of melancholy and some of pleasing character. Our cities have been visited by fire, pestilence, and flood; and our whole State has passed through a severe monetary crisis, producing extensive failures and great pecuniary embarrassment. We have lost many most valuable citizens by that modern scourge, the cholera, which for the first time visited our shores during the past fall. Under all these untoward circumstances, our population has rapidly increased, our wonderful resources have been greatly developed, and improvements have everywhere marked the progress of an energetic people. California has been admitted to her equal station among the free States of our great Confederacy; and her Senators and Representatives are now heard in the National Councils. We have great reason to be grateful to Him, who, in his wisdom and kindness, mixes the evil with the good, and scatters thorns as well as flowers along the path of national and individual existence.

The application of California for admission into the Union gave rise to bitter and long protracted discussions in both branches of Congress, such as had never before been witnessed in that body. The fearful state of passionate excitement that followed these criminaltions and recriminations, at one time seriously threatened a dissolution of the Union, and called forth the patriotic exertions of the great statesmen of all parties.

The people of California in forming their Constitution, in the simplicity and sincerity of their hearts, had supposed that they had adopted the most unobjectionable and effectual mode to allay excitement in reference to the question of slavery. They had acted upon the long established and well known principles of the South, that slavery was 'simply a domestic institution, with which the

APPENDIX

General Government had nothing to do, and which must be either prohibited or permitted by each State for herself. In the exercise of their right to form a Constitution for themselves, not repugnant to the Constitution of the United States, they had prohibited slavery within the limits of the State; not supposing that they should thereby give offence to any portion of their fellow-citizens of other States.

Perhaps in the varied history of all mankind there has never occurred an instance of such rapid and surprising progress in all that constitutes true independence and greatness, as that made by the American people under the blessings secured by that great charter that makes us one nation. From distant, oppressed, and dependent colonies, we have risen, in the short space of three quarters of a century, to the front rank among nations. We have now a secure foothold upon the shores of the Pacific; and a new ocean, and a more extended and brilliant career lie open before us, if we shall only have the wisdom and energy to improve the advantages of our position. To be harassed, under such circumstances, with civil discord at home, is most unfortunate indeed. Although our present state of national greatness and felicity might possibly have been attained without the Union, still it becomes a wise and prudent people to let more than well done alone; and this they have done, and will continue to do.

The events through which our country has recently passed have again proven the virtue and intelligence of the American people, and conclusively shown their ardent and unfaltering attachment to the Union, and to Liberty. If our people born in Republican America—well accustomed to self-government, and unshackled by old and long established monarchical institutions and customs, interwoven with all the frames of society—should yet, under these most favorable circumstances, be unable to preserve the Union and perpetuate our free institutions, then it would afford a melancholy but conclusive proof that republican systems of government are, in their very nature, impracticable and transitory; and the friends of human happiness and freedom could indulge but one regret, that our fathers wasted their blood and treasure for a purpose so delusive, and that there exists a solitary record in the world to show how much they were mistaken.

The portentous state of things that existed six months ago, it is hoped, has passed away for ever; and our fellow-citizens of every section of our country, once more united in the bonds of fraternal kindness, are ready again to march forward in the path of improvement, progress, and greatness. California will be ready to do her part. She will readily forget the opposition made to her admission, and her people will not remember the aspersions cast upon their motives and character; but she will ever be foremost in all efforts to secure prompt, equal, and exact justice to each and every section of our country. She will know no North, no South, no East, and no West, but only our whole country; and if she has been the innocent but unfortunate cause of an excitement deeply to be deplored, she will henceforth make amends to the Union by her devotion to it, by her love of justice, and by the spirit of conciliation and kindness she will ever exhibit towards all her sister States. From her distant but commanding position—separated as she is from all local causes of excitement—she will be able, and always willing, to exert a great and salutary conservative influence in the legislative councils of the country.

Since the adjournment of the Legislature, repeated calls have been made upon the Executive for the aid of the militia to resist and punish the attacks of the Indians upon our frontier. With a wild, mountainous frontier of more than eight hundred miles in extent, affording the most inaccessible retreats to an Indian foe, so well accustomed to these mountain fastnesses, California is peculiarly exposed to depredations from this quarter. The various small tribes upon the confines of California have no political organization, and no regular government among them. The influence their chiefs have over them arises from that personal popularity gained by superior prowess in war, or wisdom in council. There is therefore no reason to suppose that there has been any regular or well understood combination among them to make war upon the whites. They are all, however, urged on by the same causes of enmity; and the result has been, that at almost all points upon our widely extended and exposed frontier, hostilities more or less formidable have occurred at intervals, and many valuable lives have been lost.

Among the more immediate causes that have precipitated this state of things, may be mentioned the neglect of the General Government to make treaties with them for their lands. We have suddenly spread ourselves over the country in every direction, and appropriated whatever portion of it we pleased to ourselves, without their consent, and without compensation. Although these small and scattered tribes have among them no regular government, they have some ideas of existence as a separate and independent people, and some conception of their right to the country, acquired by long, uninterrupted, and exclusive possession. They have not only seen their country taken from them, but they see their ranks rapidly thinning from the effects of our diseases. They instinctively consider themselves a doomed race; and this idea leads to despair; and despair prevents them from providing the usual and necessary supply of provisions. This produces starvation, which knows but one law, that of gratification; and the natural result is, that these people kill the first stray animal they find. This leads to war between them and the whites; and war creates a hatred against the white man that never ceases to exist in the Indian bosom.

This state of things, though produced at an earlier period by the exciting causes mentioned, would still have followed in due course of time. Our American experience has demonstrated the fact, that the two races cannot live in the same vicinity in peace.

The love of fame, as well as the love of property, is common to all men; and war and theft are established customs among the Indian races generally, as they are among all poor and savage tribes of men, as a means to attain to the one, and to procure a supply of the other. When brought into contact with a civilized race of men, they readily learn the use of their implements and manufactures, but they do not so readily learn the art of making them. To learn the use of new comforts and conveniences, which are manifestly superior to the old, is but the work of a day; but to acquire a knowledge of the arts and sciences, is the work of generations. Like the people of all thinly populated but fertile countries, who are enabled to supply the simplest wants of nature from the spontaneous productions of the earth, they are, from habit and prejudice, exceedingly averse to manual labor. While the white man, attaches but little value to small articles, and consequently exposes, them the more carelessly, he throws in the way of the Indian that which is esteemed by him as a great temptation and a great prize; and as he cannot make the article, and thinks he must have it, he finds theft the most ready and certain mode to obtain it. Success in trifles but leads to attempts of greater importance. The white man, to whom time is money, and who labors hard all day to create the comforts of life, cannot 'sit up' all night to watch his property; and after being robbed a few times, he becomes desperate, and resolves upon a war of extermination. This is the common feeling of our people who have lived upon the Indian frontier. The two races are kept asunder by so many causes, and having no ties of marriage or consanguinity to unite them, they must ever remain at enmity.

That a war of extermination will continue to be waged between the races, until the Indian race becomes extinct, must be expected. While we cannot anticipate this result but with painful regret, the inevitable destiny of the race is beyond the power or wisdom of man to avert.

Situated as California is, we must expect a long continued and harassing, irregular warfare with the Indians upon our borders, and along the emigrant routes leading to the States. Although few in numbers, and unskilled in the use of fire-arms, they seem to understand well the advantages of their position; and they consequently resort to that predatory warfare most distressing to us, and secure to them. They readily flee before any considerable force called out to meet them, and retire to their haunts in the mountains, where it is vain for us to pursue. As time is to them of no value, they can readily content themselves to lie in wait for weeks, at secure points, ready to attack small parties of miners remote from assistance. From their irregular mode of warfare, and the features of the country in which they wage it, there is reason to believe that they will prove far more formidable than has generally been supposed; and that in the end we shall lose man for man in our encounter with them.

Considering the number and mere predatory character of the attacks, at so many different points along our whole frontier, I had determined in my own mind to leave the people of each neighborhood to protect themselves, believing they would be able to do so, and that a regular force would not find employment in the field. In two instances only have I deviated from the rule I had laid down for the government of my own action. In these cases the attacks were far more formidable, and made at points where the two great emigrant trails enter the State. These attacks occurred at a period when the emigrants were arriving across the plains with their jaded and broken down animals, and them destitute of provisions. Under these circumstances, I deemed it due to humanity, and to our brethren arriving among us in a condition so helpless, to afford them all the protection within the power of the State. I was well satisfied that the Indians would direct most of their efforts against the emigrants, as they would readily learn that they could be more successful in such attacks; and that if successful in the beginning, these attacks would be annually renewed, and the emigration of each succeeding year more and more exposed to robbery and murder. It occurred to me that it was the wisest and most humane policy, under the circumstances, to afford prompt assistance at the commencement of this system of plunder, and thus give the Indians a timely check, which would be at least likely to exert a salutary influence over them for some time to come. Had it been once known to our fellow citizens east of the Rocky Mountains, that the Indians were most hostile and formidable on the latter and more difficult portion of the route, where the emigrants themselves would be the least capable of self-protection, and that the State of California would render no assistance to parties so destitute, the emigration of families to the State across the plains would have been greatly interrupted and retarded. With all our efforts, we may expect in a few years to see all the tribes between this and the western borders of Missouri hostile, and engaged in a regular system of plunder and murder. The opportunities and temptations are too great to be long withstood by these destitute and wandering people.

The first of these attacks was made on the 23d day of April last, at the confluence of the Gila and Colorado, where Glanton and a party of thirteen men had established a ferry across the latter stream. The attack was preconcerted, sudden, and so unexpected and successful, that eleven of Glanton's party, including himself, were killed on the spot, and only three were able to escape, one of whom was wounded. It is possible that Glanton's party may have been guilty of some impropriety that gave immediate offence to the Indians: but the true motive no doubt arose from that jealousy which the Indian entertains of the white man, and which would naturally be aroused by the establishment of a ferry near the point where the Indians had a ferry of their own across the same stream. However this may be, the attack was excessive and unjustifiable, and amounted to a decided and serious act of war.

The papers communicating intelligence of this melancholy event, consisting of the sworn depositions of the three men who escaped, the proceedings of a meeting of the people of San Diego, and a letter from the Hon. Abel Stearns, Judge of the Court of First Instance for Los Angeles, were received at the seat of government on the 23d May, during my temporary absence at Sacramento City. On the first day of

June orders were issued to the Sheriff of San Diego to call out twenty men, and to the Sheriff of Los Angeles for forty, who were directed to rendezvous at Los Angeles on the 22d June, or as soon thereafter as practicable, and were placed under the command of Maj. General Bean. Subsequently the number was increased to one hundred men. Gen. Bean was instructed to let the company select its own commander, and to direct "the officer in command to proceed promptly to the ferry upon the Colorado, and pursue such energetic measures as might be necessary to punish the Indians, bring them to terms, and protect the emigrants on their way to California." He was also instructed that when the objects contemplated should have been accomplished, the company should be discharged; and that much must be left to the discretion of himself and the officer in command, which they would have to use according to circumstances. Subsequently I learned from unofficial sources that the Indians had not proved so hostile to the emigrants travelling the route as had been anticipated—that troops of the United States would be sent to the scene of disturbance, and that the expedition had failed from the impossibility of procuring the requisite number of men. I received no official report from General Bean, which I supposed was owing to the distance and the difficulty of communication; and under the circumstances, I did not then deem any order from me to disband the troops either proper or necessary.

From a communication written by General Moorehead on the 15th August, and addressed to the Hon. Richard Roman, and received by him about the first September, I was led to the belief that a party of militia were in the field under his command. I immediately issued an order to Maj. Gen. Bean, dated September 4th, to have them disbanded. All the orders issued by me to that officer, I am informed from private sources, were received by him; and yet I have received from him no official report in reference to the expedition.

The other instance in which I deemed it my duty to order out a portion of the militia of the State, occurred in the County of El Dorado, in the vicinity of Ringgold. From a communication written by William Rogers, Sheriff of that county, and dated the 23d of October, 1850, addressed to the Executive, as well as from other sources, it appeared that the Indians had sent off their women and children— had assembled in considerable numbers, and had killed several miners, and wounded and robbed several of the emigrants. On the 25th October I issued an order to William Rogers, directing him, as

APPENDIX

Sheriff of that county, to call out two hundred men armed and equipped; to cause them to assemble at as early a day as practicable, and when assembled to permit them to elect their own commander. The officer in command was instructed to proceed to punish the Indians engaged in the late attacks in the vicinity of Ringgold, and along the emigrant trail leading from Salt Lake to California. He was further directed to afford all the assistance in his power to the emigrants and others travelling the route, and not to keep more men under command than might be indispensable to accomplish the object intended; and to disband them at the earliest day when the same should be accomplished. Under the call of the Sheriff some two hundred and fifty men were mustered into service, who elected William Rogers as their commander. Not having authorized the call but for two hundred men, and not deeming the services of the others necessary, I refused commissions to the officers of the last company received into service by Maj. Rogers.

The forces were divided by Maj. Rogers into smaller parties and sent in different directions, and had different skirmishes with the Indians, in which some sixteen of their number were killed, and three of Major Rogers's command—the brave Col. McKinney, Dr. Dixon, and a Delaware Indian.

On the 15th November orders were issued to Maj. Rogers to reduce his command to one hundred men, and to make a further reduction whenever circumstances would justify such a step. This order was promptly obeyed; and subsequently, as I learn from unofficial sources, the remainder of the troops were disbanded by Maj. Rogers.

Although the troops were not able to accomplish any brilliant achievement, owing to the features of the country and the character of the foe, still they performed some hard service, and their efforts have secured peace in the vicinity, and protected the wearied emigrants. Had no determined resistance been made, the Indians would doubtless have become emboldened from this apathy, and would most likely have committed depredations far more serious.

In my former message to the Legislature I recommended the necessity and propriety of excluding free persons of color from the State. I then expressed the opinion that there was but "one of two consistent courses to take in reference to this class of population—either to admit them to the full and free enjoyment of all the privileges guaranteed by the Constitution to others, or exclude them from the State." Subsequent observation has but confirmed this opinion.

I am aware that it is a subject of great delicacy, and one that cannot be touched without exciting the prejudices and sensibilities of men; and yet it is a question that must of necessity be met, and should be calmly and justly considered. While the Legislator should entertain the most enlarged and liberal views, and should act upon all questions without hostility or partiality for or against any class of the community, he is still forced by a desire to accomplish practical good to respect the honest prejudices of men, which are not in his power either to mitigate or remove.

Our Constitution excludes this class of persons from the right of suffrage, and from all offices of honor or profit under the State; and our laws exclude them from serving on juries, and from appearing as witnesses against a white man. Although it is assumed in the Declaration of Independence as a self-evident truth, that all men are born free and equal, it is equally true that there must be acquired as well as natural abilities to fit men for self-government. Without considering whether there be any reason for the opinion entertained by many learned persons that the colored races are by nature inferior to the white, and without attaching any importance to such opinion, still it may be safely assumed that no race of men, under the precise circumstances of this class in our State, could ever hope to advance a single step in knowledge or virtue. Placed by our institutions and our usages (stronger than law) in a degraded and subordinate political and social position, which but reminds them at every step of their inferiority, and of the utter hopelessness of all attempts to improve their condition as a class, they are left without motive to waste their labor for that improvement which, when attained, brings them no reward. However talented, wise, and virtuous, they are not permitted to enter the race for fame; and if they should acquire wealth, not being permitted to testify against a white man even in a criminal case, they are left in many cases without actual protection, to be plundered with perfect impunity. They have no ideas and no recollections of a separate national existence—no alliance with great names or families—no page of history upon which are recorded the glorious deeds of the past—no present privileges—and no hope for the future. To expect any race of men thus situated to make any sensible improvement as a class, is the wildest dream of the imagination, and utterly incompatible with all our sober experience.

APPENDIX

That there are excellent and intelligent persons of color is doubtless true; but our legislation must regard them as a class, and not as individuals. While our laws professedly admit all of this class to reside in the State, they are so framed as effectually to exclude the better portion; for surely there can exist no intelligent and independent man of color, who would not promptly scorn the pitiful boon we offer him of a residence in the State, under conditions so humiliating.

The practical question then arises whether it is not better for humanity, and for the mutual benefit of both classes, that they should be separated? Is it not better for the colored man himself? I am sure, that were the question put to the more intelligent portion of this class, they would unhesitatingly say at once: "Either give us all the privileges you claim for yourselves, or give us none. Make us equal, or keep us separate." As all experience has demonstrated that it is for the mutual benefit of the parties to separate even husband and wife when they cannot live happily together, so it is the best humanity to separate two races of men whose prejudices are so inveterate that they never mingle in social intercourse, and never contract any ties of marriage.

If the measure recommended can be justified in the State of Ohio, there are still more powerful reasons applicable to the peculiar condition of California. We have here a mixed population from all the world. We have here the Southern man, with his particular opinions and feelings in reference to this class, and the Northern man, with opposite sentiments and usages; and the presence of this people among us has already resulted in death in some instances, and will continue to produce a state of embittered feeling between our fellow-citizens from different portions of the Union, and prevent that cordial unanimity so necessary to the happiness of our community. As was anticipated, numbers of this race have been manumitted in the slave States by their owners, and brought to California, bound to service for a limited period as hirelings. We have thus, in numerous instances, practical slavery in our midst.

That this class is rapidly increasing in our State is very certain. If this increase is permitted to continue for some years to come, we may readily anticipate what will then be the state of things here, from what we see now occurring in some of the free States. We shall have our people divided and distracted by those distressing domestic controversies respecting the abolition of slavery which have already produced so much bitterness between different portions of the Union. When those who come after us shall witness a war in California between the two races, and all the disgraces and disasters following in its train, they will have as much cause to reproach us for not taking timely steps, when they were practicable, to prevent this state of things, as we now have for reproaching our ancestors for the evils entailed upon us by the original introduction of slavery into the colonies. We have the warning voice of experience—they had not.

I would call the attention of the Legislature to the propriety of amending the twenty-first section of the eleventh article of the Constitution, which provides that "all laws, decrees, regulations, and provisions, which from their nature require publication, shall be published in English and Spanish."

This provision of the Constitution must remain in force under every change of circumstance until amended, and the Legislature can exercise no discretion, but is forced to carry it out in its true spirit and intent. The necessity and propriety of publishing the laws in Spanish, it occurs to me, should have been left to the judgment and liberality of the Legislature to be governed by circumstances, and should not have been made a permanent Constitutional provision.

From the best estimate I have been enabled to make, the translation of the present statutes into Spanish, and their publication in that language, will cost the State from forty to fifty thousand dollars. It is difficult to procure correct translations, and so many delays have occurred in publishing them in that language, that they are not yet ready for distribution. When distributed they will impart very little information to those for whom they are designed, for the reason that the statutes form but a small portion of the law that affects the daily transactions of business. The great mass of every community do not derive any knowledge of the law from the reading of statutes, but from intercourse with intelligent men, and especially from witnessing legal proceedings in Court. These must necessarily be in English, as they cannot be in both languages. We have now, or soon will have, as many citizens in the State who alone speak the French or German language as we have of those who speak the Spanish. To publish all the laws in all these different languages would be almost impracticable. Besides it would be of very doubtful utility. To speak the one common language forms a strong tie between citizens of the same State, and so long as the laws are published in different languages, so long one great incentive to learn the prevailing language is taken away, and the causes of a separation of different classes of our fellow-citizens must continue.

I would earnestly invite the attention of the Legislature to the urgent necessity of amending the criminal laws of the State in several particulars. The original criminal jurisdiction in cases of felony is confined to the District Courts. These Courts are only required to hold certain terms in each county at different periods of the year, with long intervals between. There are very few prisons in the State, and the expense of detaining prisoners from one term to another is exceedingly oppressive upon some of the counties; and these circumstances, joined to the impossibility of procuring the attendance of witnesses in cases where the trials have been delayed, have rendered the administration of the Criminal Laws of the State, especially in the mining counties, almost wholly impracticable. As administered, our laws have afforded no protection to the innocent, but have given great encouragement to offenders. Some more prompt, decisive, and efficient mode of enforcing the Criminal Laws of the State must be adopted, or the great ends of criminal punishment cannot be attained. I would, under the circumstances, suggest the propriety of conferring criminal jurisdiction upon the Courts of Sessions for some of the counties, requiring them to hold frequent regular terms and also called terms at any time when necessary to try a criminal, and giving the right of appeal as in other cases.

The punishment generally inflicted by our criminal statutes in cases of felony not capital is fine and imprisonment. These punishments taken together, or singly, for very obvious reasons, have little or no practical effect under existing circumstances. I would therefore recommend that other modes of punishment be adopted. For grand larceny and robbery I would suggest the punishment of death. This severe punishment I would not recommend as a permanent one, to be continued when the State shall have her county prisons, and her penitentiary; but such has been the frightful increase of these crimes since the adjournment of the Legislature that I know of no other mode of punishment, under present circumstances, that would be at all likely to check the evil, and prevent our citizens from taking justice into their own hands. The crime of grand larceny, in stealing horses and cattle, has become so common, in many places, as to diminish their value fifty per cent. In some instances whole bands of tame cattle have been stolen, and farmers have lost all their teams, and been compelled to abandon their business in consequence. A firm and determined stand should be taken by the Legislature, and all the good citizens of the State, to extirpate these prevailing crimes. In the early periods of new communities, it has often been indispensably necessary to adopt more severe modes of punishment than would be justifiable in better regulated and older States. The State of Tennessee was infested, at an early day, with bands of horse thieves, and she was forced to adopt capital punishment in such cases; and a few years' rigid and prompt execution of the law effectually checked "the commission of the crime.

By an act of the Legislature parties to contracts are allowed to bind themselves to pay any rate of interest they may agree upon, and the Courts are bound to enforce the contract. In support of the principle involved in this measure, it has been often urged that money is but an article of commerce; and that, as such, if lenders have a right to charge any interest for the use of it, they surely have the same right to stipulate as to the rate to be charged as the landlord who rents out a house or a farm; and that the law has no right to interfere, but should enforce the contract in the one case as promptly as in the other.

However simple and apparently unanswerable this plausible theory may be, all experience has demonstrated its ruinous practical effects upon communities; and therefore it must be wrong in principle. I apprehend the error consists in considering money as simply au article of commerce, when it is in truth a standard of value, made so by law, and must be received in satisfaction of all debts.

The credit system itself is sufficiently dangerous, but when connected with an extravagant and unlimited rate of interest, produces irreparable ruin to a large portion of the community. Few men rightly calculate the legitimate effects of paying a high rate of interest for money. If an individual borrows a considerable sum of money at a high rate of interest, and should not be able to pay it when due, the accumulation of a few months' interest puts it for ever beyond his power to pay. He sees himself ruined for life—makes no further efforts to pay—leaves his creditor to sustain the loss of both principal and interest, while the borrower himself becomes a hopeless idler, and from thenceforward a useless, if not an evil member of

APPENDIX

society. If each individual stood alone, unconnected with others, there might be some truth in the principle assumed. But the State has an interest in the protection of individuals, as the prosperity or ruin of individuals makes up the prosperity or ruin of the whole. If a practice be injurious to public morals, or public policy, it is the right of the State to restrain it.

The idea that competition among lenders would reduce the rate of interest to a fair and just standard, such as the legitimate profits of business would justify; seems to be delusive. Our own sad experience in California has conclusively shown that competition among lenders does not diminish the rate of interest; but the rates now asked, and the amount of security now demanded, are equal to, if not greater, than those required one year ago. I cannot but express the opinion that the late monetary crisis in California has been more the legitimate result of the oppressive rates of interest charged than of any other one cause. The result in many, if not in most cases, has been ruin to both lenders and borrowers. If the system is permitted to continue for some years longer, the productive industry of the State will be seriously crippled.

By the act of the Legislature in reference to Notaries Public, the Executive is authorized to appoint as many Notaries for each county as he may deem necessary. As Justices of the Peace are not empowered to take the acknowledgments of deeds and other instruments, having no seal with which to authenticate the same, and as Notaries only reside in the towns and cities, it is exceedingly inconvenient for persons at a distance from the residence of a Notary to procure the authentication of instruments, especially where females are parties. It is difficult for the Executive to know what number of Notaries may be required for each county, and more difficult for him to know the character and qualifications of the applicants; and when appointments are made, the incumbents change their residence so frequently that it is almost impossible to keep a sufficient number in office in some of the remote counties. I would therefore suggest that the law be so amended as to require Notaries Public to be elected in the same manner as Justices of the Peace, and required to reside in their respective townships; the number to each, township to be determined by the County Court, or the Court of Sessions.

In pursuance of the act authorizing the Executive to appoint Commissioners of Deeds, appointments have been made for many of the States, the incumbents to reside at the principal commercial points. To appoint a Commissioner for each county in every State in the Union would be a laborious task, if not impracticable at this distance; and yet where appointments are made at only one or two points in each State, people who reside at a distance from the Commissioner would be compelled to incur much expense before they could avail themselves of his services. It is difficult for the Executive to know the character and qualifications of the different applicants, especially as those most meritorious are not always the most active in procuring recommendations. These officers when appointed are not subject to the control of the State authorities where they reside, and they are beyond our reach, and practically irresponsible for any malfeasance in office; and the present system must, in the end, lead to great abuses.

The laws in the different States in relation to taking and certifying the acknowledgments of instruments and the depositions of witnesses, are substantially the same; and if the effort were made in a spirit of enlightened liberality, it is thought that a uniform law upon these subjects might be adopted by the different States, containing the same provisions in reference to instruments and depositions to be sent out of the State. This system, if once adopted, would avoid the evils of the present one, and afford much greater facility and security for the transaction of this kind of business. The law might be so framed as to be operative between all the States adopting it; and a few years experience would demonstrate its practical benefits, and thus ultimately secure its adoption by all. It would form another link in the golden chain that binds together the States. California has a special and particular interest in this matter, at this period of her history, as her people are from every State in the Union, and have left behind them friends, relatives, and property, in almost every village and neighborhood in the Republic.

The beneficial effects of a system of direct taxation have already been seen in the increased impulse given to our agriculture during the past year. The large tracts of land have, in many cases, been subdivided, and smaller portions sold to agriculturists, who have thus become permanent and prosperous residents. The agricultural resources of California are much greater than have usually been supposed, and are equal to those of most of the States. In the language of one of her most intelligent citizens, "her fertile valleys and rich prairies are capable, when cultivated, of producing an untold store of agricultural wealth."

In pursuance of an Act of the Legislature defining the duties of the Surveyor General, it was expected that that officer would be enabled to embody in his report much useful and statistical information in reference to the geography and agriculture of the State. For reasons stated in his report, he has not been able to do so. This information would have been exceedingly useful in the present infant state of that branch of industry. The climate and soil of California are peculiar, and the mode of cultivation best adapted to them is consequently very little understood. The result has been that the most incorrect views have been entertained by most persons in reference to these matters. While the opinion has generally been indulged that irrigation was indispensable to the success of the farmer, the past year's experience has shown that all the grains and nearly all the garden vegetables can be grown in great abundance without it.

Were it not for the fact that our State is embarrassed in her finances, I should recommend the establishment of a separate and distinct Bureau of Statistics; but as the duties of the Surveyor General are not so onerous as to prevent his attention to this subject, and as they are, from their nature, somewhat connected with it, I would recommend the continuance of the provision requiring him to collect information from the different County Surveyors.

In connexion with this subject, I cannot but express my regret that the Legislature (owing to a difference of opinion as to the best mode) failed to carry out that wise and humane provision of the Constitution, which was designed to protect from forced sale a certain portion of the homestead of all heads of families. This provision is peculiarly appropriate to California, and is another evidence of the wisdom and enlightened liberality of the framers of our excellent Constitution. Without families it is impossible for any State or community to exist and prosper. This provision, if carried out in the same enlightened spirit in which it originated, and especially if followed (as it is hoped it will be) by an Act of Congress making grants in limited quantities to actual settlers upon the public lands, will soon fill up our State with energetic, industrious, and virtuous families, who will thus secure a permanent home, not dependent upon the fluctuations of trade and business. There can be no doubt but that the practical operation of this just and liberal provision will be eminently beneficial to both debtors and creditors, as it will have a tendency to check the excesses of the credit system, and to make the credit of individuals, as it should ever be, more dependent upon their integrity, capacity, and industry, than upon the amount and value of the property they may temporarily control.

I may deem it my duty to call the attention of the Legislature to the necessity of a general reduction in the salaries of officers whose compensation is fixed by the Legislature. It is not in the power of the Legislature to reduce the salaries of most of the present State officers during their continuance in office; but any reduction made will affect their successors.

The present rate of compensation, as fixed by the last Legislature, was perhaps too high under the then existing circumstances; but however that may be, since that time a great reduction has taken place in the prices of labor, both manual and professional, in property and rents, as well as in the expenses of living, and a corresponding reduction, it would seem, should be made in salaries. It is contrary to the genius and simplicity of a republican Government, to pay extravagant salaries. While an officer should be allowed such compensation for his services as will afford him a plain, decent support, he should not be allowed such a salary as would amount to a speculation, in a case where there is no risk incurred. The opinion entertained by many that high salaries will secure the services of men of superior merit is not correct in all cases. High salaries excite more the cupidity of men than their patriotism; and more of that class succeed in obtaining office, when salaries are high, than when they are at a fair rate. When salaries afford a certain but only a moderate living to incumbents, their duties are discharged with an eye to the approbation of their constituents, and to the acquirement of honest fame, motives more powerful in securing a faithful discharge of official duties than the desire of high salaries.

In this connexion I would suggest the propriety of reducing the fees of clerks, recorders, and other officers. The rates at present allowed are exceedingly oppressive upon those who seek justice in our Courts.

Cheap and speedy justice is one of the cardinal maxims of Republican Government: but when the Courts are only open by the payment of exorbitant costs in advance, it is better for men to suffer wrong than to seek redress.

At the late general election there was elected a Superintendent of Public Instruction. It will be necessary to pass an Act prescribing his duties and fixing his compensation. Under existing circumstances, before any of the public lands to which the State will be entitled have been assigned to her, and while we have so few families in the State, and our population is so unsettled, it may not be practicable to establish any general system of free schools, or to endow any university. But the time must soon arrive when we shall have both the families and the means to adopt and carry out such a system. In the meantime it might be made the duty of the Superintendent to collect useful statistical information, to be reported annually to the Executive, and by him laid before the Legislature at each regular session.

By the provisions of the second section of the ninth article of the Constitution, "all estates of deceased persons, who may have died without leaving a will or heir, shall remain a perpetual fund, the interest of which shall be inviolably appropriated to the support of common schools throughout the State." It would be wise to make some efficient provision by law for the security of such funds, and for lending them out by responsible officers. I would recommend that they be deposited in the State Treasury, and invested in State securities.

I take great pleasure in referring to the passage by Congress, at its late session, of the Act granting the swamp and overflowed public lands to the several States in which they may be situated. By this law the State of California will be entitled to immense bodies of fertile land bordering upon the bays of San Francisco, San Pablo, and Suisun, and upon the rivers San Joaquin and Sacramento. These lands, it is thought by many intelligent persons, when properly drained and cultivated, will produce bountiful crops of rice, and perhaps of sugarcane.

For the want of the necessary surveys and plats, no estimate approaching towards accuracy can be made as to their extent and quantity, and a considerable time must elapse before their limits can be defined. It will be expedient for the Legislature, at au early period, to adopt some permanent line of policy in reference to the disposition to be made of these lands, and the proceeds arising from them, after deducting the necessary expenses of the levees and drains.

Without the passage of this Act, the right of eminent domain which resides in the State would entitle her, upon general principles, to all the lots in the City of San Francisco, covered by ordinary high tide, so soon as the same should be reclaimed from the dominion of the sea. By this Act, however, every doubt may be considered as removed; I would, therefore recommend that these lots be ceded to that City upon such conditions as may be just. I would also recommend that the right of pre-emption be granted to actual settlers upon these lauds, on such equitable and liberal terms as may best promote their rapid improvement and cultivation.

Under the Joint Resolution authorizing the Governor to procure a suitable rock, to be contributed by the State to the Washington Monument, I caused notice to be published in the public prints, asking information and soliciting proposals from individuals. Having received no proposals, I found it necessary to employ a special agent for this purpose. The agent employed was William L. Smith, Esq., who proceeded to the South Mines, and succeeded in procuring a beautiful specimen of gold-bearing quartz, from the quarry of Messrs. Jackson and Elliston. It was placed in the care of the Hon. John Bidwell and Henry A. Schoolcraft, Esq. I cannot but mention, in this place, the generous liberality of Messrs. Howland, Aspinwall & Co., who transported the rock from San Francisco to New York City, and Messrs. Adams & Co., who conveyed it from thence to Washington, free of charge. It was there delivered to our delegation in Congress, who delivered it to the President of the Washington Monument Association.

The past year has witnessed the rapid improvement of our cities, and the increasing development of our great commercial resources. Our trade with all the world, and more especially with China, the Islands of the Pacific, and the northwest coast of America, has greatly increased in amount and importance, and our principal commercial points have already assumed the beautiful forms of regular cities. The people of California are destined to become a great commercial people; and every obstacle that has a tendency to shackle and trammel commerce, without a corresponding benefit, should be removed by the Legislature, so far as that body may have the power. With this view, I recommend an entire repeal of the act establishing quarantine regulations at San Francisco. These regulations have proved a vexatious burden to commerce, while they have been impotent for good. I would also recommend a thorough revision of the act creating a Marine Hospital and a Board of Health at that point. I would also recommend the repeal of the act establishing the Superior Court of that city, and the passage of an act creating additional District Courts. The people of San Francisco not only pay their proportion of revenue to support the Judiciary of the whole State, but they are compelled, in addition to this, to pay the entire expenses of the Superior Court. I take it to be clear that the people of every portion of the State are of right entitled to as many Courts, created and paid by the State, as may be required to administer justice. Where a Court is required to enforce mere local ordinances, not common to the whole State, it constitutes an exception to the general rule; but the Superior Court has as much civil jurisdiction as the District Courts, and consequently comes within the general rule.

As the law exists, it is matter of doubt whether appeals lie from the decisions of Justices of the Peace to the Supreme Court. Although the amount involved in each case tried before these inferior Courts is small, except in cases of Forcible Entry and Detainer, yet they make up in number what they lack in amount. The principles, and the aggregate amounts involved in these cases, are of as much importance to the community as those arising in civil cases brought in the District Courts. As appeals only lie to the County Courts, there can be no uniformity of decision; and what will be law in one county will not be law in another.

The late period of the session at which California was admitted into the Union, and the press of other business, occasioned by the long and protracted debates in both Houses upon the disturbing question of slavery, prevented Congress from passing acts for the establishment of a Mint at San Francisco, and for refunding to the State the duties collected in California previous to the recognition of our State government. For the want of a Mint the industry of the State has been severely taxed, and we have been forced to become tributary to other portions of the world to the amount of millions.

The act of Congress passed in the beginning of the year 1849, extending the revenue laws of the United States over California, was perhaps the most extraordinary act ever passed by that body, and was a plain and palpable violation of the most prominent principle, the disregard of which by the mother country led to the American Revolution. If there was one single principle well understood, and inflexibly cherished by the heroes of that great struggle, it was the self-evident truth that taxation could not rightfully exist without representation. In other words, that both the government and the governed have some rights, which rights are mutual, and the exercise of the one depends upon the exercise of the other; and that while it is the duty of the citizen to pay his taxes, it is equally the duty of the government, at one and the same time, to afford him protection in his person and property.

One cannot contemplate the astonishing provisions of that act without the most painful regret. It extended the revenue laws over California, not only without representation in Congress, but without giving or allowing us any government at all. The act imposed upon us burdens, but extended to us no benefits. It practically, although not in terms, placed judicial and ministerial power in the same hands; thus making the Collector of the Port of San Francisco both the collecting officer and the judge of the law, in cases in which he had a direct interest himself; and when the injured party complained, he was mocked with a delusive show of justice, by being referred to the distant and inaccessible courts of Oregon and Louisiana; a provision about as equitable and just as the practice of Great Britain in transporting our people across the Atlantic to be tried in England, for alleged offences committed in the Colonies. Not a single case, to my knowledge, among the many decisions of the Collector, the correctness of which was called in question, was ever taken to the courts either of Oregon or Louisiana, for the very plain and simple reason, that justice in such cases would have cost more than it would have been worth, when attained.

The history of all governments having colonies has shown how natural and usual it is for the mother country to oppress, and at the same time neglect a distant and helpless people. It is so natural and easy for legislative bodies, as well as for individuals, to form prejudiced and disparaging opinions of others at a distance, and thus to find pretexts for oppressive exactions, while benefits are conferred with great reluctance. The fruits of these exactions never fail to reach the seat of the oppressor, while the indignant complaints of the oppressed fade and vanish in travelling over the intervening distance, and are never heard nor regarded.

APPENDIX

The act in question forms another strong and irresistible evidence of the truth of the great republican maxim, that an oft and frequent recurrence to first principles is indispensably necessary to the preservation of our institutions in their original purity. California will always be among the most devoted to this just sentiment; and while she has the honor and happiness to remain a member of the Confederacy, she will strenuously insist that justice be meted out to her, by refunding the moneys thus unjustly collected. This she owes to herself—to her own honor—but above all to sacred principle and to the Union.

This act seems to have been passed at the close of the session, when there was not sufficient time for calm and deliberate reflection; and since the date of its passage, the attention of Congress has been almost wholly taken up with the consideration of other measures of more immediate and pressing importance. To doubt that justice will yet be done California, is to doubt the justice of Congress; and to doubt the ultimate justice of Congress, is to doubt the justice of the American people, their capacity for self-government, and the perpetuity of our institutions.

The question of revenue and expenditures, so important to individuals, families, and States, will necessarily occupy much of your attention. Of the temporary State loan there have been issued bonds to the amount of two hundred and ninety thousand one hundred dollars, of which the sum of nineteen thousand four hundred and fifty dollars has been redeemed, leaving outstanding on the 15th December, 1850, the sum of two hundred and seventy thousand six hundred and fifty dollars, upon which interest had accrued to the amount of seventy-one thousand eight hundred and thirty-six dollars and four cents, making the sum total of the State Debt created under the act authorizing a temporary State loan, amount to the sum of three hundred and forty-two thousand four hundred and eighty-six dollars and four cents. In addition to this, there were unredeemed Comptroller's warrants to the amount of one hundred and forty-two thousand nine hundred and seventy-four dollars and twenty-four cents, which, added to the outstanding three per cent. bonds, and the interest' due upon them up to December 15, would make the sum total of the State Debt on that day four hundred and eighty-five thousand four hundred and sixty dollars and twenty-eight cents. The total amount of receipts into the Treasury up to the 15th December, amounted to the sum of three hundred and twenty-four thousand nine hundred and seventy four dollars, while the expenditures up to the same period amounted to the sum of four hundred and forty-seven thousand one hundred and fifty-three dollars and eighty-five cents; leaving an excess of expenditures, over and above receipts, of one hundred and twenty-two thousand one hundred and seventy-nine dollars and eighty-five cents. The estimated receipts for the second fiscal year, ending on 30th day of June, 1851, amount to the sum of five hundred and nineteen thousand five hundred and fifty dollars; while the estimated expenditures under the present rates of compensation amount to the sum of four hundred and ninety-five thousand seven hundred and forty-seven dollars, leaving an excess of receipts over expenditures, of twenty-three thousand eight hundred and three dollars. But should the expenditures be reduced, as suggested by the Comptroller, to the sum of two hundred and eighty-nine thousand two hundred and three dollars and fifty cents, and the receipts into the Treasury equal the estimates, then there would remain a balance in the Treasury, on the 30th day of June, 1851, of two hundred and thirty thousand three hundred and forty-six dollars and fifty cents, applicable to the payment of the State Debt.

The act for the better regulation of the mines met with serious opposition in various portions of the State, and the amount of revenue derived from this source fell far short of what was confidently anticipated. Under the act there was collected and paid into the Treasury up to the 15th December, the sum of twenty-nine thousand seven hundred and thirty-one dollars and sixteen cents; and the further sum of nine thousand nine hundred and forty-one dollars yet remains in the hands of L. A. Bensancon, the former Collector of Tuolumne County.

The necessity of convening the Legislature for the purpose of passing an act to procure a loan for the State, was seriously urged upon my attention, and the subject received all the consideration its great importance demanded. Extra sessions of the Legislatures of several States, as well as of Congress, have been frequently called, and not one of them, to my knowledge, has ever equalled the expectations of its friends. The only result that is certain to follow an extra session of a legislative assembly is a heavy amount of additional expense, while the benefits are matters of doubt. In the present case, whether a quorum of both Houses could, have been obtained, admitted of some question; and whether, when assembled, a majority of both Houses

APPENDIX

could have agreed upon a bill for creating a State loan, was more than problematical.

Our Constitution only authorizes the Executive to convene the Legislature upon "extraordinary occasions;" and to guard against the abuse of this power, the Governor is required to "state to both Houses when assembled the purpose for which they shall have been convened." From this language, as well as from the nature and reason of the case, the "extraordinary occasion" contemplated by the framers of the Constitution must be some new and very important event, such as the happening of war, or other serious cause, arising after the adjournment of the Legislature, and which could not have come under its consideration while in regular session. The propriety of authorizing a loan in addition to the temporary State loan of three hundred thousand dollars, was elaborately discussed in the Legislature before its adjournment; but the bill did not pass. It is true that the State was not then admitted into the Union, but that event was confidently anticipated. It is also true, that the act imposing a tax upon foreign miners had not then been tested, and had not then failed; and the present financial condition of the State was not then foreseen. But the mere deficit in the revenue was not, in my opinion, such an "extraordinary occasion" as required an extra session of the Legislature. The condition of the Treasury of the United States, at the time President Van Buren convened Congress, in consequence of the suspension of the Deposit Banks, was certainly as critical as the present situation of our State Treasury; and yet the result proved the action of the President in that case to have been unwise and unnecessary.

But there were other powerful reasons, founded upon principle, that had their due share of influence in forming my opinion upon this question. To have effected a loan it would have been necessary to issue bonds running some fifteen or twenty years, and bearing a high rate of interest. Capitalists, knowing that the money was only wanted to defray the current expenses of the civil administration, and not for the purposes of constructing some great, permanent, and profitable improvement, which itself would probably afford the means of ultimate reimbursement, would have demanded these conditions.

The practice of contracting State debts, especially for the mere purpose of defraying the ordinary expenses of the State Government, and when these debts are not to be paid until after the lapse of years, is one of pernicious tendency and of evil example, and would seem to be a plain violation of just and honest principle. Most of the States have contracted debts for the purpose of internal improvement; but few of them have borrowed money to defray ordinary expenses. There is a vicious principle in the practice of putting our burdens upon posterity without their consent. Those who have the liberty to contract debts should bear the responsibility of paying them. It would be exceedingly convenient for individuals, as well as States, to enjoy the happy privilege of contracting debts for their own use and benefit, while the burden of their payment would be thrown upon the shoulders of others. If such a system could once be successfully adopted, it would be found so easy and so tempting that there would remain no check and no limit to the evils to be entailed upon future generations.

The expenses of the Convention which framed the Constitution having all been paid the only use the State had for the money to be obtained by loan would have been to defray ordinary and present expenses. If for instance, the State had borrowed one million of dollars, every dollar of it would have been expended to pay our present expenses, and would have saved us, of the present day, that amount of taxation; but the payment of this debt would have been postponed for years, and forced upon others against their will and without their consent, while they would have received none of the benefits and would have the expenses of the State accruing in their own time to pay besides. While we are complaining, and justly too, that Congress has taxed us without representation or government, thus imposing upon us the burdens without giving us the benefits of government, we are urged. to commit the same violation of principle, by borrowing money and expending it for our own temporary purposes, and at the same time putting the entire burden of payment upon our successors; thus in effect taxing them without bestowing any corresponding benefit in return.

It may be said that we confer benefits upon posterity, and they ought therefore to pay our debts. But it is plain that we shall confer no greater benefits upon them than those we have received from our ancestors, and no greater than they will confer upon their successors; and if we have the right to place our burdens upon them, they in their turn will have the same right to place their burdens upon the next succeeding generation; so that each existing generation, one after the other, will have the right to borrow money to defray their own daily

APPENDIX

expenses, and to put the task of payment upon their successors to the end of time.

Had the Legislature been convened, and a loan obtained, it would have precipitated the State into a system of extravagance which would have been difficult to lay aside. In two years from this time, the State would have been in a condition as much embarrassed as at present, if not in a worse condition. There can perhaps no greater misfortune befall a young State, than a large surplus in the treasury produced by a loan. It puts the people and the government upon delusive hopes, and starts a system of expenditures that cannot be sustained and continued. Young States, like young and inexperienced individuals, never cease expenditures while there is money in the treasury; and seldom stop while they have any credit left. The time must come when the State expenditures must fall within the limits of her income, and the sooner this is brought about the better for all parties in the end. It would, perhaps, be best for her to adopt a system of rigid economy at the commencement, so as to be certain to come within their limits.

As the Legislature has now no Constitutional power to borrow money, and as there are no cash funds in the treasury, the question arises how the current and necessary expenses of the State are to be paid. I would recommend that the present rate of taxation upon real and personal estate be continued, and that a reasonable reduction be made in the rate of the capitation tax. This latter tax has been generally considered too high, and this feeling has materially diminished the amount of revenue expected from that source. Were the rate less, a much larger amount could be collected. I would also recommend that Comptroller's Warrants be made by law receivable in payment of all State dues; and that the law requiring that officer to draw these warrants be amended, as suggested by him in his able report. These warrants may fall below their par value, but being made receivable in payment of the State dues, they will be absorbed by the incoming revenue, and this circumstance will facilitate the collection of taxes, and prevent any great depreciation in the value of the warrants. If the whole amount issued should be less than the amount of the State revenue, then they will rise nearly if not quite to par value. To bring about this desirable state of things, I recommend a rigid system of retrenchment in the expenditures of every department of the State. It occurs to me that the most rational, just, and certain mode of getting out of debt, is to make more, expend less, and borrow none. I also recommend a reduction of the rate of taxation imposed on property sold at auction. A larger amount of revenue can be collected from this source, it is thought, were the rates reduced. As at present established, the rates are so high as to materially diminish the amount of sales.

The attempt to administer the State Government during the past year has been attended by many difficulties. To start a new system, under ordinary circumstances, is no easy task,—but no new State has ever been encompassed with so many embarrassments as California. Our people formed a mixed and multitudinous host from all sections of our widely extended country, and from almost every clime and nation in the world, with all their discordant views, feelings, prejudices, and opinions; and thrown together like the sudden assemblage of a mighty army, had no time to compare notes or interchange opinions. Besides this, a Majority considered themselves only temporary residents, and had therefore no permanent interest in sustaining the State Government. Serious resistance to the execution of the laws was threatened in some instances, and a very unfortunate disturbance occurred at Sacramento City, in reference to which it would be improper to express an opinion, as the facts of the case will be inquired into by the competent judicial tribunals.

The first session of the Legislature had more difficulties to meet than perhaps the Legislature of any other State. That body had no beaten road to travel, no safe precedents to follow; California required a new system, adapted to her new and anomalous condition. What that new system should be, time and experience could alone determine. With the experience of the past year before us, we may be enabled to make some useful and necessary amendments. I have suggested such as have appeared to me the most important. It will be doubtless necessary to amend the acts of the last session in many other respects; but I would respectfully suggest the propriety of making no amendments except where manifestly required. The people have now become accustomed to the laws as they are; and by making but few amendments a heavy amount of expense may be saved to the State.

The report of the Comptroller, herewith submitted, contains many valuable suggestions, to which I would respectfully invite your attention.

APPENDIX

In conclusion, I would make but one other suggestion, more important than any yet made, because it concerns the virtue and honor of our community. The fourth section of the first chapter of the "act to regulate proceedings in civil cases," is in these words:" Sec. 4. No action shall be maintained for criminal conversation or for seduction."

I recommend an entire repeal of this section, that the law may throw around the chastity of our wives and daughters that protection which ought to be afforded by the laws of every civilized country in the world.

San Jose, January 6, 1851.   PETER H. BURNETT.

Index of Names

A

Alemany, Joseph Sadoc, 17
Anderson, Associate Justice 31, 34, 35
Applegate, Jesse 70, 89
Applegate, Linsey 71
Archy see Archy Lee

B

Baines (Judge) 170
Bancroft, Hubert Howe 38
Barclay, (Doctor) 88
Bates, Frank 114, 115
Bean, J. H., Major General 21, 131, 132, 133, 135, 221
Bellows, Henry Whitney 159
Bennett, James Gordon 6, 61, 68, 73, 78
Bensancon, L. A. 237
Benton, (Colonel) 117
Bigler, John 39
Birch, W. F. (editor) 49, 51, 54
Blackstone, William 25
Botts, Charles 28
Brannan, Samuel 114, 115
Breckinridge, John 146
Brown, John 174
Brownson, Orestes J. 18, 155, 156, 165, 170
Brownson, Sarah 156, 165
Buffom, E. Gould 122
Burnett, (Long, Cain) Elizabeth A. 192
Burnett, (Poe) Sallie C. 18, 185
Burnett, (Ryland) Martha L. 185, 186, 199
Burnett, (Smith) Constantia 9

Burnett, (Wallace) Romeetta J. 185, 199
Burnett, Armstead L. 18, 143, 185
Burnett, Dwight J. 185, 186, 199
Burnett, George 9
Burnett, Glen 186
Burnett, Harriet see Harriet Rogers
Burnett, John M. 143, 169, 186, 193, 199
Burnett, Thomas 186
Burnett, White 186
Burnett, William, 186
Burrill, George T. 131, 133

C

Cahill, Daniel William 153, 158
Campbell, Alexander 13, 15, 26, 149, 157
Casan (Mr.) 70
Celsus, 160
Ciccateri, Felix 149
Cist, L. J. 144
Clinch, General 12
Cole, Paxton 191
Congiato, Nicholas 145
Covarrubias, José Maria 41, 132

D

Davy, Humphrey, Sir 84
De Vos, Peter 15, 146
DeGenat, (Mr.) 156
Dixon, Dr. 222
Dulany, 61
Dulles, Avery Cardinal 7, 37

E

Edmonds, John 95

INDEX

F
Field, Stephen J. 32, 33
Forbes, John M. 159
Fowler, John S. 115

G
Gadsden, James 30, 32
Gant see Grant
Gilbert, Edward 122
Glanton, John Joel 222
Gordon, Robert 115
Grant, John 62, 70, 77, 83
Gray, William Henry 38
Green, Thomas 30, 31

H
Hal, (Uncle) 25
Hardeman, Blackstone 10
Hardeman, Constant 9
Hardeman, Dorothy 9
Hasaszthy, Agoston 131, 133
Hittell, Theodore 39
Howard, William D. M. 122
Hughes, Andrew S. 55
Hughes, James M. 97
Hughes, John 146, 159, 162
Huntington, William Reed 157
Huntington, Frederick, Rev 165

I
Ives, Levi Silliman 159, 160

J
Jackson, Andrew, President 12, 20, 21
Johnson, Adam, Colonel 23
Juarez, José 23

K
Kenrick, Francis Patrick 160, 162
King George III 42

L
Lapp, Rudolph M. 32
Lassen, (Lawson) Peter 15, 108
Lee, Archy 30, 32, 33
Lee, Barton 114
Lincoln, Abraham, President 25, 28, 41, 42, 43
Lippitt, Francis J. 43

M
Maritain, Jacques 42
Marshall, Linsay 185
Martin, William 70
May, David W. 199
McCarver, Morton M. 14, 89
McCown see McCarver
McHealy, 61
McKinney, Colonel 222
McLouglin, John 20, 89
McPherson, John C. 196
Meek, Joseph L. 95
Mullaly (Mr.) 159
Murray, Hugh 31

N
Nesmith, Jim 69
Nobili, John 146
Noland, (Mr.) 71
Norton, Myron 122

P
Pakenham, Richard 96
Pappa (Frenchman) 68
Pay, M. 12

INDEX

Peck, W. Blount Rev. 10
Perkins, C. S. 31
Polk, James K., President 4, 14, 119
Priest, Albert 114
Purcell, Edward 160, 164
Purcell, John Baptist 15, 149, 152, 153, 159, 162, 166, 169, 179

R

Reading, P. B. 115
Rice, Nathan Lewis 157
Ridge, John Rollin see Yellow Bird
Rigdon, Sidney 12
Riley, Bennett C., General 16, 121, 123, 124, 125
Rogers, (Burnett, Mrs. B.) Harriet 10, 11, 13, 18, 26, 78, 96, 169
Rogers, Peter 10, 11
Rogers, William 136, 137, 138, 139, 223, 224
Ryland, Adele 185
Ryland, Caius Tacitus 156, 194

S

Saint Augustine 151
Saint Paul 36, 155, 163, 164
Saint Peter 163, 166, 167, 169
Savage, James 23
Scott, Dred 30, 32
Seward, William H 179
Shannon, William 28
Sister Loyola, (Sisters of Notre Dame) 158, 168, 170
Smith, Joseph 12
Smith, William L. 235
Smith, William, Major 9
Socrates 5
Springer, (Mr. and Mrs.) 154, 160, 164, 168, 170
Starkie, Thomas 120

Starr, Kevin 7
Stearns, Abel 220
Stephens, Calvin 10
Stovall, Charles 33
Sutter, John 16
Sutter, John A. 16
Swartz, George 63

T

Taney, Roger B. 30, 34
Taylor, Zachery 116, 117
Terry, David 32, 33
Thompson, General 12
Titus (Roman Emperor) 155
Turnham, Joel 95
Turnham, May 95

V

Van Buren, Martin, President 12
Voegelin, Eric 3

W

Wall, Kevin 3
Wallace, Romeetta See Burnett
Wallace, W. T. 194
Ware, J. M. 62
White, E. 91, 93
Whitman, (Whitmarsh) Marcus 61, 83, 101
Wight, Lyman 12
Wilkes, George 6
Winn, A. M. 134, 136, 137, 139
Wiseman, Nicholas Cardinal 160
Wood, James Fredrick 160

Y

Yellow Bird (John Rollin Ridge) 19, 20
Young, Fredric 6

www.ingramcontent.com/pod-product-compliance
Lightning Source LLC
Chambersburg PA
CBHW021057080526
44587CB00010B/278